The Unveiling of The Divided States of America

Introduction to the two competing parties:

The Insane vs. The Stupid

(808) 276-1005

XULON PRESS ELITE

BUT WAIT...

THE CRAZY COURAGEOUS PARTY

IS RISING TO TAKE OVER

Xulon Press Elite
2301 Lucien Way #415
Maitland, FL 32751
407.339.4217
www.xulonpress.com

Unless otherwise indicated, Scripture quotations taken from the
New King James Version (NKJV). Copyright © 1982 by Thomas
Nelson, Inc. Used by permission. All rights reserved.

Printed in the United States of America.

Paperback ISBN-13: 978-1-6322-1452-2
eBook ISBN-13: 978-1-6322-1453-9

DEDICATION

D edicated to all who will fail the insanity and stupidity tests: all who are of the nameless minority who are bravely standing in the gap until the rest of us come to our senses.

Let's join them and rise up and form a third party...the Crazy Courageous...to restore the United States of America.

Wake up, rise up and take back your country!

"the price of liberty is eternal vigilance."
-Thomas Jefferson

FOREWORD

I began to write this book before the Covid-19 pandemic started. I was just about finished when the sudden world-wide shutdown began. It was like the pulling back of the tarp, revealing the skeletons of our divided nation. It put an exclamation to my concerns. This book was not meant to be political but to just expose the philosophical influences that were making changes in our American way of life. I was hoping to arouse sleeping Americans.

I thought it may be like Paul Revere's famous, "the British are coming, the British are coming," call made famous by Henry Wadsworth Longfellow's legendary poem, "The Midnight Ride of Paul Revere".

However, I now must declare. "They are here. The disguised enemies of our great America are here…no longer disguised!!!" The Civil War is on! We are seeing it every night on our evening news. Frightening, isn't it?

Like most Americans, I thought that the political problems and differences we had were internal…we Americans just drifted apart as we perceived things differently because of our natural diversity.

The more I researched, the more I realized that most Americans of Generation X and the Millennials, did not have a good education on government and history. Politics was for the "professional" politicians. Plus, most Americans rarely drift away from their family's political heritage. They did not notice how the platforms of the different parties had evolved over the years.

I hope you read on because what I discovered is that the Marxists, who had hopes to take the world and establish their one world government, had specific plans to use unconventional tactics to defeat America. They knew they could not defeat us militarily so they patiently and surreptitiously crept through our universities, bonded with the poor and discouraged, infiltrated our church's social programs and organized groups so they could get elected to our government's high offices.

It is frightening but what you see on your nightly news are the fruits of their patience and our ignorance. Their plan to divide and conquer is so evident that it could not be by accident:

black against white
female against male
rich against poor
the law-abiding against the lawless
the Godly against the ungodly

The race wars, the disarming of Americans, the loose immigration laws, more dependence on federal government handouts, the burning of our cities and the intimidation of our policemen are fulfilling plans made nearly a hundred years ago in Russia and Europe. A Venezuelan, seeing the tearing down of our national monuments and the desecrating of memorials of our Founding Fathers, has sounded the alarm. Will we learn from Venezuela or remain stubborn and stupid?

They cleverly made us turn on each other so they don't need an army to invade us. They are using us to destroy each other.

Because the Marxists were godless, they chose to work with the party which favored godlessness.

My hope is that you will reassess your political will and agenda. I believe we can outsmart them and stand together to make America great again.

I am screaming out so sleepy compliant Americans will wake up. Our enemies look like Americans, they are dressed like Americans, they talk like Americans but if you stop for a second, you see that they are fueled by godless animosity for the American way of life. They are enemies of our God and country. I realized that this fight was no longer a political one. I don't think even the staunchest Democrat realizes what has happened. I don't think the Democrats have any platform anymore but to divide, hate and riot.

We clearly see it in the women's revolution. Who can forget the well-staged outcry from our Senator from Hawaii telling American men to shut up in the sacred chambers of our Capitol building. It was very sad to see her do that because it is so against our culture.

The race card is being used to justify riots fueled by George Soros-sponsored paramilitary professionals who never wasted a crisis. Yes, they have their own militia! Antifa began in Europe and is now imported to destroy us. George Soros, by the way, is a Hungarian billionaire who was thrown out of his own country. Why do you think they are working so hard to disarm us?

Deep racial prejudice against the blacks birthed the abortion industry to "help them have a better life," not realizing that to poor people, even as they struggle, their babies are their joy and comfort, their security and help for their old age. Family was important to them.

Because the vultures hate is disguised as compassion, they indoctrinate blacks teaching them that they are "entitled" to get things without working. They pass programs that keep them poor and dependent, and satisfied to eat the crumbs.

Think about this! Since the Civil Rights act of 1964, nearly 60 years ago, have the lives of black Americans improved? For some, it has. But most of them in inner cities still are looking for handouts. They should look at the boat people of Vietnam. They fled their war-torn country in boats and eventually arrived in America. Within about a dozen years or so, many were millionaires. Their secret? A lot of hard work and families helping each other get ahead. We have some on Maui and I have watched them prosper.

If community organizing projects worked to better the lives of blacks, why in Chicago, where it started, are more blacks killing blacks than police killing blacks? If gun control laws work, why are there so many murders there every week? Note the dates: between 2014-2016, the murder rate in Chicago nearly doubled. The sad thing is that they were freed from one form of slavery and then were seduced into another more sinister slavery. If you want your city to be like Chicago, keep voting for those who make it possible.

What upsets me is that this deception and feigned empathy, robs these beautiful black people of dignity, and their true American dream. Their leaders should empower them by teaching them that they are Americans first, and black, second. Yes, we are all proud of our cultural heritage but in America, we are Americans first.

Did you notice when a President, a former community organizer from Chicago was elected mainly because he was black, we have had more racial problems?

Taking the bait and going the route of people who admittedly use anger as a political force, they have subjugated themselves to the enslavement these deceivers have designed for them. The vultures applaud when rioters burn down businesses, and when they challenge, intimidate and kill law enforcement officers. This serves as fuel for more hate and anger. They have made a huge bonfire that practically feeds itself. And they are smiling.

The strength and insights of the blacks that injustices of suffering produced by God's grace, have been overshadowed by the desecration of the memory of our American hero, Dr. Martin Luther King. If blacks had chosen to follow the path he paved, I believe General Colin Powell or former Secretary of State, Condoleezza Rice could have easily become President of the United States, if they had chosen to run. The amazing thing about these two is that most people didn't see them as black or white, male or female. They could have won on their own merits and accomplishments. That is how it should be!

When blacks choose not to be victimized, they have so much to enrich our nation. The soulful music that kept them close to the God of their comfort, is a gift to our nation. Appropriately played on the black keys of the piano, they anchor our soul to God. There's no preacher that can preach like a black preacher. They have insights that we who have not gone through their kind of pain, can ever articulate as powerfully and eloquently as they can. I lived in the South in the early 1960's so I can appreciate the power of their messages.

If you are still wondering if the destruction of America is planned, what if I told you that in a pasture in Elberton, Georgia, a few miles where my alma mater Emmanuel college is, stands the mysterious monument, "Georgia Guidestones," erected in 1980.

The capstone reads, "Let These Be Guidelines To An Age Of Reason". There are ten guidelines written in eight languages for humanity's post-apocalyptic age. The most controversial is the first guideline which says that "Humanity should be under half a billion in perpetual balance with nature." (the world's population at present is 7.66 billion.)

What if I told you that the morass of the Middle Ages in Europe gave birth to the Renaissance Humanism and the Age of Reason. The absolute monarchial system and the fixed dogmas of the corrupt church hierarchy made the educated think that they must find a solution to change the oppression. Since the church was not giving hope, they decided that there must not be a God and man had to discover his own way to make humanity function.

The invention of the Gutenberg press in 1438 opened the way for mass communication. Books could be printed, and information shared. Clubs and societies were formed to discuss different ideas. The Protestant Reformation that began around 1519 discovered untruths in the religious world. Man's traditions and thirst for power had compromised the Word of God. Religious hierarchy had intermarried with the aristocracy and the Church's influence was diminished.

What if I told you that, "The Age of Reason, Being An Investigation of True And Fabulous Theology," was written by Thomas Paine in 1794? He was a British and American activist. His writings reflected British deism. He denied that the Bible was a sacred, inspired text and argued that Christianity was a human invention. Thus, human reasoning became God.

He inspired the free thinkers, both in Europe and America. Benjamin Franklin and Thomas Jefferson, among others, before and after the American revolution, were influenced by his writings.

His writings were also the inspiration behind the secretive Illuminati movement which was dominated by the banking family headed by Mayer Amschel Rothschild. This wealthy Jewish family originally from Frankfurt, Germany soon dominated and controlled most of Europe's money.

The Illuminati have influenced the Freemasons, the Marxists, the Communists, the Fascists, and it crept into the United States with various innocuous sounding names like socialism, liberalism, progressivism, and ideologies that are "politically correct."

Their enemies became those who believed that being "Biblically correct" was the foundation of our nation and should stay that way. Hence, the great war we are now engaged in. Is this not the same battle from the beginning of time:

good vs. evil,
life vs. death,
God vs. the devil?

Now it seems like it's also female vs. male!

To the "Biblically correct," we believe that there is an eternal power smarter, and wiser than man, to whom we are accountable.

"There is a way that seems right to a man, but its
end is the way of death."
Proverbs 14:12

If there is no God to the "politically correct," he can reason to do what is right in his own eyes…a free thinker, and accountable only to himself. There is a warning for that,

> "Woe to those who are wise in their own eyes,
> and prudent in their own sight!"
>
> Isaiah 5:21

Our Declaration of Independence has ideas coming from those influenced by Paine, the ideas seem "reasonable" and noble. But when God is left out, we always find that man's ways fall short. (Did you notice that every great invention man has made has negative side effects?) Read the disclaimers on your medication. Or do you remember the barge which floated up and down the East Coast because there was no place to dispose of the wonderful disposable diapers? Humbling, isn't it?

When the Civil Rights movement was growing and there was a lot of soul-searching, I realized that there was a major flaw in the beloved man-created Declaration of Independence. Parts have deteriorated with age. See if you can catch them!

> "We hold these truths to be self-evident, that all
> men are created equal, that they are endowed
> by their Creator, with certain unalienable rights,
> that among these are life, liberty and the pursuit
> of happiness."

Let's start with truth…. I don't think we can use that word because in America our justice system no longer seeks or honors truth but seeks to outwit the opposing side and win. Winning is more important than truth. Americans love winning.

What about "endowed by their Creator"? The Scopes trial in 1925, led the nation to accepting that the Creator was overthrown in favor of the monkey. Americans like having an excuse to act like a monkey.

Unalienable rights? I have witnessed that in giving rights to one group, it inevitably takes away the rights of another. Do you remember that they had school busing to help kick-start school desegregation? But they soon found out that it was an insane plan to take kids across town to get their education.

I saw almost immediate reverse discrimination when I was living in the Washington, D.C. area. At that time, some of my white friends at church received early retirement notices to make room for young minority people without experience to take their jobs. I was urged to stay and seize the opportunity to start near the top since I was a minority. I refused because I knew it was not right.

Do you know the pain of reverse discrimination? A hard-working American working toward his American dream and looking forward to a well-deserved retirement, but because of his age and the color of his skin, suddenly loses his job and his dream. I saw the tears and consider them heroes for not complaining or rioting. We never discuss that.

We saw the unfair way chef Paula Deen was treated when she was accused of using the "N" word nearly 20 years before. Her career and life were turned up-side down in days. Why were so many silent?

Blacks have derogatory words they use against the whites, but we never discuss that. What I could not understand is that they can use the "n" word with each other and hope to eliminate it from our vocabulary.

Is it any wonder that the seeds of bitterness from their injustices would motivate the wounded groups of whites to rise-up and fight? Those who fight for "black lives matter" shouldn't be so hard on the White Supremacists. It is the same hate and anger against injustices but in a different color. They are as senseless as each other.

To those who are promoting hate to "better" our nation, I ask, "where does the cycle of hate end?" If you watch the evening news, you see that we are ending in an incendiary heap. How proud of that are you? You may feel like you are not a part of that insanity, but if you refuse to fight it, you contribute to it by your silence. We must be determined to resist the temptation to succumb to evil.

What about the right to life? Oh, that was thrown out in 1973 with the Roe vs. Wade decision. About 60 million unborn Americans never saw daylight. So, watch out, those of you who want to live. It has been turned around to a "right to die" situation and they will set traps for you when you are on the slippery slopes of vulnerability. But, when there is no God, there is always the spirit of death.

The one, I think, that has affected our nation the most is a noble but unbiblical one..."that all men are created equal".

Have you been to a maternity ward and seen the newborns? Some are 2.5 pounds, and in an incubator. And another about 12 pounds and ready to eat a watermelon.

What about the cemetery? Headstones show that they were not equal in time spent on earth.

What about those born blind or crippled or poor?

Do you know how many lives could have been saved if only two words had been added? A half a million Americans would not have been killed in the Civil War alone.

We are not born equal, but we are born <u>Of Equal Worth.</u> Man saw man as equal, but God made man of equal worth. That is the big difference between how man thinks and how God values us.

"But God demonstrates His own love toward
us, in that while we were still sinners, Christ
died for us."

Romans 5:8

We would not have had race wars, gender wars, religious
wars, class wars had we understood that. You know, we could
have had a peaceful nation. But, of course, if we believed that we
are of equal worth, we would need to love each other. Therefore,
no God means no love because God is love.

Now, do you understand why there is so much hate, and
so incumbent on those of us who believe in God to operate in
love? Think about that! The courageous will have to take the
challenge and follow the examples of the following who showed
this seething nation, how to seize the opportunity and show
how it's done. These are my heroes.

It was a peaceful Wednesday Bible study night, June 17, 2015.
Evil in its vilest form came disguised and sat with about a dozen
faithful attendees at the Emanuel African Methodist Episcopal
Church in Charleston, South Carolina. After being cordially
invited to sit and pray with them, a young White Supremacist
killed nine of them, including Senior Pastor, and State Senator,
the Rev. Clementa Pinckney.

Investigation showed that this church was chosen because
of its history and importance to the Civil Rights Movement.
How very easy it would have been to turn this horrific event into
a national riot. Instead, the grieving instinctively responded to
display the Gospel:

"Beloved, do not avenge yourselves but rather
give place to wrath, for it is written, 'vengeance

is mine, I will repay,' says the Lord…Do not be overcome by evil, but overcome evil with good."

Romans 12:19,21

In these times of senseless racial riots and anarchy sparked by the death of one man, the nation should take time to read two books that show us what our Christian faith is all about. The first is, "For Such A Time As This: Hope And Forgiveness After The Charleston Massacre", written by Rev. Sharon Risher, daughter of one of the slaughtered. The other, "Called To Forgive" was written by Pastor Anthony Thompson, whose wife Myra was also killed.

The loss of a loved one is always difficult, but to lose them in such a senseless act of hate, takes supernatural grace to overcome. Their grace and strength of Christian character saved their beautiful and historic city from disintegrating in flames.

Could they have been the inspiration to Brandt Jean? He did a similar thing in a Dallas courtroom. Only 18 years old, he faced his brother's killer who had just been given a ten-year sentence. After reading a victim-impact statement saying that he had forgiven her, he spontaneously and unprompted, asked if he could give her a hug. The courtroom was stunned, and the judge allowed him to do that.

He said his main desire was not for her to go to jail, but for her to give her life to Christ.

Who taught this young man to take his pain and anger to the cross and leave it there? Who taught him not to be common but courageous and do what was not expected, to make this world a better place, and especially lighten the burden of the one ridden with guilt?

Yes, there is a faithful momma, Allison Jean. She wrote in her Facebook page, "I am proud of you my son, Brandt. Your load is lighter. Regardless of the views of the spectators, walk with God always. Forgiveness is for the forgiver and it doesn't matter what the forgiven does with it." We need more mommas like that. We need more Americans like these who did the courageous thing when there was that temptation to be common. That is the way to outwit and outsmart the enemy from without!

What simple and profound eloquence. I am sure it took perseverance and a lot of prayer to bring up a son like that. We got to see the Botham we never got to know by what we saw his brother do.

Brandt, what a timely gift you have given to this nation that needs to know that love works. What a tribute to your family who could have set Dallas ablaze with hate, but you have set the world on fire with love. May we never forget Brandt's hug, and may we offer a hug whenever we have reason to hate.

I think Brandt deserves a full football scholarship to the biggest university. He doesn't play football you say? It doesn't matter! Let him sit on the bench and teach the others humility and the power of love! Why do we keep rewarding young people who only know how to kick and catch a ball and don't know how to appreciate the blessings they have. Someone has said that if you keep doing the same thing over and over and expect different results you are insane. So, what do you think we are? If we want our nation to change, we had better change some of our priorities.

It is amazing the impact parents have on their children. What if I tell you that the present governor of New York is the son of the late three-time governor of New York, Mario Cuomo? What if I tell you that dad Cuomo, in his early political years, was a member of the liberal/progressive party, whose main issues were abortion, increased spending on education and universal healthcare and that party was absorbed by the Democratic party of New York?

Remember the big celebration in January 2019, of the legalization in New York of the murder of babies up until birth? (even though a USA today poll shows that only 13% of Americans support the murder of babies in the third trimester of pregnancy) He lit the New York World Trade Center in pink to celebrate. Does the apple fall far from the tree in the Big Apple? I think insanity can be genetic, as well as contagious as a virus.

When this pande-mania hit us, I thought only Hawaii was insane as our leaders freed our criminals from their unaffected quarantine of sorts. Of course, nobody figured out that having no place to go and no resources, they would rob already apprehensive people and then perhaps get sent back so they could infect the safe ones.

I quickly learned that insanity is not only in Hawaii. I think it travels very fast and is highly contagious if you hang around certain parties. I think I will ask Dr. Fauci, since I heard he is so popular, his bobble head is outselling others and now is a member of the bobble head Hall of Fame. He seems very smart.

In New York, did you think it strange that the Governor would send Covid-19 patients to nursing homes when we were all told at the very beginning that the elderly were the most vulnerable? Oh, how shocking that nursing homes had such high number of deaths and became known as "clusters," while the Governor feigned concern and grief.

While medical staffs were overworked and hospitals were reportedly overcrowded without enough ventilators and other medical supplies, something insane was happening.

It happened so fast that it seemed like a blur. After doing research for this book, I realized that vultures were prepared to take advantage of the blur. You will understand why I unkindly call those in the blur, stupid. When you look up the definition, you will understand and hopefully, will want to step out of the blur into sanity, if you are guilty.

In New York, which was hard hit, the Governor called for help. The Navy hospital ship USNS Comfort was dispatched and transformed to accommodate 1,000 patients and had 1,100 on their medical staff, recruited from many military facilities. These were put in accommodations elsewhere to make room for the expected flood of patients. It treated a total of 182 patients from the time it docked on March 30 and left on April 26, not quite a month.

An article by Michael Schwartz on April 2 in the New York Times, reported that the 1,000-bed facility with its 1,100 staff had 20 patients. A top hospital executive whose facilities were packed with coronavirus cases said, "It's a joke".

A nurse from a hospital in Harlem who wished to be anonymous said that out of 95 applicants they wanted to send, only one person passed the 25 guidelines they had to pass in order to qualify for admission. Yikes, I think we can relinquish our crown and hail New York as the most insane state in the nation!

By April 14, in New York City alone, there were 110,000 covid-19 cases.

On March 20, Javits Convention Center was converted to be a field hospital in four days with the help of FEMA. It was able to accommodate 1,000 patients in its first phase. Another 1,500 beds were added later. The total number treated was about 500, according to one report. After millions of dollars were spent setting it up, it closed on May 1.

If it doesn't scare you that we have allowed politics to weave its power to manipulate health issues and give fake news a field day, I have other things to do that.

Would it surprise you that medical students take the most popular modernized medical oath at graduation, "pledging to take responsibility not just for the person's health, but for how the illness affects a person's family and economic stability?" It is called the Lasagna Oath after Dr. Louis Lasagna, former dean of Tufts University School of Medicine.

No wonder when my elderly mother was weak but not in pain, she was greeted with a disdainful, "Oh, it's you again!" The elderly should be aware that if they need your hospital bed you may be politely asked if you would like to make an exit to the next world, especially if you have some pain. They will tell your relatives that they are only prolonging your pain, if they insist that they would like for you to have continued treatment. I have heard that speech myself at the bedside of some of my parishioners.

What if I told you that there is something scandalous that is happening in the vaccine world? Did you know that Robert F. Kennedy, Jr. is crusading against mandatory vaccinations? When he was holding hearings on the dangers of mercury in our environment, he met too many parents who brought their autistic children telling him that the child had been completely normal until taking vaccinations which had mercury in it. His investigation shows four pharmaceutical companies…Merck, Pfizer, Sanofi U.S.A., and Glaxo-Smith-Kline were producing these vaccines and making billions of dollars. They were also allegedly making billions of dollars producing the pills that "cure" these ills. How insane is that!!

Recently, Kennedy was interviewed on Daystar Television on Joni Talk Show. He said that he was glad to be on the show because ever since he started this research he has been shut off by CNN and the other liberal media. He reported that doctors were alarmed that the Center For Disease Control's protocol was pressuring them to put Covid on the death report. They were receiving from Medicare $13,000 for every Covid death and $39,000 for everyone who had been put on the ventilator. How insane is that!

He has researched Bill Gates' control in the World Health Organization and his association with the now famous Dr. Anthony Fauci. Through their programs, they have vaccinated thousands of children in Africa with vaccines that are not allowed in the United States and many have died.

In describing Bill Gates, he said that he has a Messianic belief that he was ordained to be bring salvation to humanity through technology. He said that Gates did not recognize that God gave human beings an immune system that was most miraculous and that it can heal itself. Bill Gates thinks that only technology can save us and that he is the genius that can supply it.

For more information, look at his website, childrensheath-defense.org. or on Instagram: Robert F. Kennedy, Jr.

He works closely with Del Bigtree, founder of ICAN and the Emmy-winning host of "The High Wire with Del Bigtree," which streams every Thursday at 11 a.m. (PST) on YouTube, Facebook, Twitter and thehighwire.com.

Their studies show that the Center for Disease Control has falsified data, bribed doctors, and lied to the public. The previously mentioned companies have been criminally indicted 113 times and fined $33 billion but allowed to continue to go on without hardly any supervision or accountability.

Dr. Stanley Alan Plotkin, an American physician who works as a consultant to vaccine manufacturers, has admitted under oath that fetal tissue and other horrible ingredients are used in some of these vaccines. Under oath he also admitted to being an atheist so is it surprising?

Each state has its own regulations. In Hawaii, children entering school must have had nine vaccinations. When they enter the 7th grade, they are required to take 3 more, including HP (Human Papillomavirus). This vaccination which has not been properly tested is given to the girls to prevent cervical cancer. While that may prove to do so later, one of the side effects is that some are contracting autoimmune diseases that are horribly degenerative and there has been an increase of suicide among them. Does anyone care?

In the fall of 2020, our Health Department has already announced that there will be additional immunization requirements for all students.

At my age I know I will not be dying young, but I don't want to be mandated by the government to be immunized to get on an airplane. That means that I will have to spend the rest of my life going around in circles on Maui! Can't you hear their argument? It will not only be for your safety, but to prevent you from passing something to somebody else! You must think about others.

What was Italy's attitude when they were hit hard by this coronavirus? They announced right off that the hospitals were overcrowded and that they were not going to treat the elderly.

The innocent or ignorant may be surprised at what is happening to America. But hell is where God is not, so where God is not, can you see what we have become?

These insane evil deadly systems are already in place. I hope it will arouse us all, not to only elect a God-fearing President, but a Congress to support him. We are tasting the spirit of death all around us. In America, we have the power to stop evil by voting it out of office.

Our State leadership must be God-fearing, too. For our children's sake, I feel that young parents should consider running for office, starting from the school board. It may be the most important thing you can do for your children, besides going out to vote courageously.

We are at a tipping point and if we don't wake up, our nation will literally burn up.

I hope disbelieving politicians would take a short trip to Europe and see what it has become. Foreigners don't want to become a part of the country they come to live in. They want to establish their own culture, religion, and judicial systems like the Sharia courts that Britons are now having to contend with. In the past, we used to have to go to war to prevent that from happening. Now, we fight among ourselves to let them in. How insane is that!!!

Although some of the seeds were already in the foundation of our country, we have been assigned by God, I believe, to be warriors to push back the spirit of godlessness in our country for such a time as this.

My inspiration comes from Andy Andrew's book, the New York Time bestseller, "The Butterfly Effect." This book explains the law of sensitive dependence upon initial conditions. In short, it means that a butterfly could flap its wings and start molecules moving to later start a hurricane on the other side of the planet. As incredible as it sounds, Edward Lorene presented this hypothesis to the New York Academy of Science in 1963. Thirty years later, a physics professor confirmed it.

In Andrew's book, you will learn that one courageous, audacious act of a Maine schoolteacher-turned soldier, Joshua Lawrence Chamberlain during the Battle of Gettysburg, made the United States of America…and the world, what it is today.

One desperate act of compassion by one farmer's wife in Diamond, Missouri when Missouri was still a slave state, has saved the lives of billions of people living in drought-stricken areas around the world.

So here I go, fluttering my butterfly wings. I hope you will flutter yours too. We've got serious business to do…defeat the godless, angry, hate-filled disillusioned army, so America can be great again.

However, before I go on, I want to put out a disclaimer. I learned what a disclaimer was when I saw one on our local T.V. station. In effect it said that it didn't want to be responsible for the contents of the following program, just before my pastor friend's inspirational program. The only other one I have seen here is before the 700 Club which also gives hope and is uplifting. They don't put disclaimers before the violent Hawaii-5-0 and other more violent and vulgar shows that I have noticed. So since my book will hopefully give hope and be an inspiration, I want to put my disclaimer out.

Disclaimer: none of my relatives or friends, organizations, or the church I am affiliated with, any political organization or person, is responsible for the content of this book. I, being of a sound mind (my opinion…you decide) have tried to put together information I have stored up, read about or googled (I hope they don't pull out some of the articles I used) for such a time as this. These are my own thoughts and personal opinions. I do this of my own free will, not having gotten funding from anyone except my own social security checks. It has cost me nearly a year of my checks and at least a year's worth of my time. Maybe I am crazy!!! You decide! I hope you read on to find out.

INTRODUCTION

I have a persistent friend who for years urged me to write a
book. Since I was an expert on nothing, her persistence meant
nothing. However, in the fall of 2018, she came with a blank
book, thrust it into my hands and said, "this is the year to write
your book".

She is the wife of a theologian/professor and they have
been my friends for over 50 years…since our college days in
Georgia. All our inner circle friends know that when Frances
gives you that look and gives you a command, you stand at
attention…and pray.

With that blank book in hand, I wondered what I would
be able to write and appear to be intelligent. Then, the Brett
Kavanaugh confirmation hearings started to consume the attention of the United States of America. Something churned in me
and I could not sleep. I knew that something was wrong, ter-
ribly wrong.

As I assessed the state of our country from my vantage point
in the middle of the Pacific Ocean, I wondered why I should
even consider writing a book. Hawaii is the 4th smallest in the
nation in land area, the 40th in population and the last to be

admitted to the United States of America. Our islands are the farthest from any land mass…about 2,500 miles.

However, as I reflected on my life, it seemed that my life has been orchestrated to experience extraordinarily important events. I had been allowed to hear intriguing conversations and meet amazing people, perhaps, for such a time as this.

I lived in the south and Washington, D.C. in the early 1960's. I was in Washington, D.C. when Martin Luther King gave his famous "I have a dream" speech on the steps of the Lincoln Memorial.

When President John F. Kennedy's body was brought back from Dallas, I drove up with friends to Washington and waited in Lafayette Park across the White House. We watched as limousines brought foreign dignitaries to pay their respects. Later, we stood with thousands as his funeral cortege brought him from the White House to the Capitol.

I had my spiritual roots deepened at Emmanuel College in Franklin Springs, Georgia. I earned a bachelor's degree in history from East Carolina University (then, still a college), in Greenville, North Carolina. My summers and school breaks were spent in the Washington, D.C. suburbs. I was an eyewitness to the changes that the civil rights movement was making in our nation.

My parents, as most of their generation in Hawaii, were loyal Democrats. My grandparents from Okinawa, Japan, were immigrant laborers. My parents and their generation were afforded an education that helped better their lives. But they were quite unaware of their political power until a former policeman, John A. Burns, made them realize the power of unity of ordinary people in America. He helped organize and solidify the Democratic party by convincing the working class that they can rule Hawaii. Until then, the big-5 landowners ruled the Republican Party and the state.

His efforts paid off. John Burns won the second gubernatorial election after statehood. He strengthened the party's hold on Hawaii politics. Nearly all the congressional and local political offices were held by the Democrats. Although it improved the living standards of the workers, he did not foresee how the impact of people from different ethnic and religious backgrounds would affect the moral climate of Hawaii. He may not have realized that he was also inviting a sinister virus that was beginning to affect our nation.

Hawaii has a wonderful and rich Christian heritage. Soon after Captain James Cook "discovered" the Hawaiian Islands in 1778, traders began to stop by and introduce the world to Hawaii. They brought in goods, trinkets, tools and mosquitos, mice, and diseases and the like, that Hawaiians had not had before.

In the 1800's, the first missionaries from New England brought Christianity to Hawaii. Among them were doctors who helped save the Hawaiian population from different plagues of infectious diseases with their knowledge of inoculation. Their teachers translated the Bible into Hawaiian and taught them to read. In a few years, Hawaii became the most literate nation in the world. It had the world's largest Protestant church in the world with over 10,000 members in Hilo's Haili Church.

In 1827 the first Catholic priests came from France and Ireland. Hawaii was known as the most Christian nation in the world at that time. Tribal warfare ceased and the sanctity of life was practiced as native Hawaiians abandoned the practices of cannibalism and human sacrifice.

On January 17, 1893, there was a coup d'etat against Hawaii's beloved and godly monarch, Queen Lili'uokalani. A republic was formed with the intent of annexing Hawaii to the United States. That happened in 1898. Through that tragic event, many Hawaiians began to drift back to their pagan faith.

I am so grateful to be living in Hawaii and on Maui, chosen by tourists as the most beautiful island in the world and the most desired travel destination, at one time.

I come from an extremely patriotic family perhaps because of our deep spiritual roots, and because my father almost died on the battlefield in Italy. During the 2nd World War, he, like many young men from American Japanese families, fought to defend, not only their country, but the loyalty and integrity of their American families who were being persecuted because of their racial background. He received a Purple Heart and a Bronze Star as a member of the famed 100th Battalion and the 442nd Infantry Division which was the most highly decorated of the war.

In the spring of 1959, I was in my junior year of high school. All class activities stopped and Baldwin High School's intercom system, like others around the islands, broadcast the countdown toward Hawaii's statehood from the floor of the United States House of Representatives. The Senate already had passed its bill the day before and President Dwight Eisenhower was waiting to sign it into law. When the vote that got us over the top was cast, we screamed with joy. Classes were dismissed and spontaneous celebrations broke out everywhere. It was doubly exciting for me because it was my birthday!!

Knowing that we now had full rights as American citizens was the best birthday present. Several years later, I was interviewed with the nephew of President Eisenhower. He was a resident of Washington, D.C. and was opposed to making the District of Columbia a state. A Puerto Rican television reporter wanted our opinion on the issue of statehood because it was a big issue at that time in Puerto Rico. Although I was very enthusiastic for statehood, he was evidently more convincing.

Sadly, in 1970, not too long after statehood, Hawaii became the nation's first state to pass the abortion on demand law. John Burns was governor. But, as a Catholic, it became law without his signature.

In the Honolulu Star Bulletin on March 21, 2000, reporter A.A. Smyser quoted him as saying at that time,

> "I have declined to sign this bill after much study and soul-searching, after receiving competent advice from mainland and national specialists in law, medicine, theology, human rights and public affairs, and also sincere prayer to the Creator named in our Declaration of Independence as the source of our inalienable rights of life, liberty and the pursuit of happiness."

Tiny, faraway Hawaii, whose native culture loves children, led the nation in this moral travesty. Sadly, the culture that loves children is being victimized by the evils of abortion and they are producing fewer and fewer Hawaiians.

Progressives who have wanted to change the moral climate of our country have used us in issues like gay rights and marriages, physician-assisted suicide, and the brilliant idea of total mail-in voting!!!

The saddest part of this is that many religious leaders either don't know what is going on or are just refusing to speak out…..and our nice comfortable Christians have chosen godless candidates over God-fearing people who want to change the spiritual climate of Hawaii! In Hawaii, we say, "auwe!!"

My parents were never silent about their stand for God and country. When my father became pastor, he established a practice on the first Sunday of the month of singing a patriotic song, saying the Pledge of Allegiance to the flag and praying for our country and President. Even now, although he has been gone nearly 30 years, we still continue that tradition.

On Memorial Day, before we go on our picnic, we take our youth to the Makawao Veterans' Memorial Cemetery. We stand around the flagpole, pledge the flag, sing "God Bless America", say a prayer of thanksgiving for our heroes, put leis on the graves of members of our church who are buried there. Then, we go and enjoy our picnic.

Being Pentecostal, we don't have many traditions, but they felt that the church is the best place to teach the generations to maintain important Godly ones.

My love for my country is strong. When I see these insane things that are corrupting our American way of life and wasting so many lives, the warrior spirit in me wants to respond.

The more I thought about it, I wanted to honor the memory of my courageous dad. I think he would want me to rise up against the insanity that is overtaking our island, state and country in the undeclared Civil War that is going on. He would be proud of me using my social security money to do it!

I know he would think it insane to bottle our free delicious water and pay more for a gallon of water than for a gallon of gas. But, what about the other insane things that are destroying our country?

Tragic statistics, some affecting my own extended family, compel me to do something.

1. Suicide rates have nearly doubled since 2000. In 2017, five-thousand sixteen males and one-thousand two-hundred twenty-five females between the ages of 15-24 years took their own lives. And the rate has been

rising every year. I had a cousin on drugs who committed suicide.

2. The sad status of families: half of marriages break up (over 2 million a year). Pew Research Center reports that the U.S. has the highest rate of children living in single parent households. In an article published by Erin Duffin on January 13, 2020, roughly 19 million children live in a single parent home. My cousin was divorced from his beautiful wife and left two sons when he took his own life.

3. Opioid addiction: The National Institute on Drug Abuse report that 128 people die of drug overdose every day in America. It costs the government $78.5 billion every year to cover the cost of drug addiction including addiction to pain killers and other prescription drugs.

4. A report from Bradley University on the mental health of America reports that 47.4 percent of Americans will experience a mental health problem during their lifetimes. Many live with forms of depression. Many of the homeless in our neighborhoods are mentally ill. Recently, outside my office was an elderly lady bent over in her wheelchair. I asked her name and if I could help her. She lifted her head and yelled at me, "shut up, you smart aleck." Because she was in pain, I called 911 and the police and the EMS people came. They all knew her. She did not want their help and even refused to go to a shelter. She was eventually taken to a park where she seemed to be comfortable. How sad. Homelessness will increase as drug addiction and mental health problems increase. This is a growing problem in every American town. Trying to fix this problem is like filling your leaky bucket while the holes get bigger. How very sad is that!

5. The National Alliance to End Homelessness reported in 2017 that 553,742 people were experiencing home-lessness on any given night. The organization feeding America reports that there are 41 million Americans going hungry every day. Thanks to our good weather, some come with a one-way ticket to paradise which some states reportedly give to get rid of them.

6. In 2014, the Guttmachjer Institute, a pro-choice and research organization reported 926, 200 abortions, about 2,537 a day in our nation. Are we smarter and richer when we destroy our most precious natural resource...our children? Is not this a moral pandemic... a crisis, greater than the covid-19? I call it insanity.

7. The rise of violence. We are not safe in malls, restaurants, working places, churches and our children are not safe in schools. By the time a child is 18, he will have watched twenty-thousand acts of violence in movies or tv and sixteen-thousand murders plus, all those terrible video games. We give awards for these popular shows. Should we wonder why we have so much violence? Don't blame the guns. Guns don't kill. Crazy violent people do.

8. Pornography is a blight on the nation. Sex trafficking has become an international problem. Young children are sold and abused by the insatiable, sadistic appetite of depraved people. Does it not concern you that according to Jayleen Sanders, contributor to HuffPost, that 1 in 5 girls and 1 in 12.5 boys will be sexually abused by their 18th birthday? The problem is growing and who will stop it? Not their parents because some of them are encour-aging their young children to have a sex change opera-tion! How sick have we become without God?

9. Blatant perversion of the media: we can monitor the moral health of our nation by what we laugh at and what we cry over. Pornography, violence, anger, adultery, rebellion, disrespect and dishonor flood us. How insane…are we to think that we can play them over and over all day long and they not affect or behaviors. We can learn to make a pipe bomb, network with others who share like passions and educate ourselves in whatever we want. Information may be true or not but there is no filter. Should we wonder why our programmed brains produce the painful events that are now almost commonplace in our society? Bonnie Miller Rubin in a related article in 2010, reported that young people spend 7 hours and 38 minutes on the T.V. or computer…before cell phones became the norm. Kaiser family foundation reports that 53 hours a week…more than a full-time job is spent on daily media use. And the numbers are rising.

For these disturbing facts and statistics, should we not get our heads out of the sand and ask ourselves, "Why?"

When I got my head out of the sand, I realized that the same politicians who are making outrageous promises for solutions which they don't know how to pay, are the very ones passing legislation that are creating these horrible problems. If that isn't insanity, I don't know what is. And, if we allow them to do that, we must be stupid.

Has your family been touched by any of these social and moral pestilences which have been robbing us of our wonderful American life? If yours has, don't you want to do something to restore it to become the American dream again…something that has made us the envy of the world? We cannot do it alone, but collectively we can and must!

Chapter One

FLUTTERING MY BUTTERFLY WINGS

know that some will be angry with my perceptions and obser-
vations. But, when you think that I am controversial or insane,
let me tell you why I have a right and obligation to speak out
in this Civil War which is destroying our families and nation.

I know pastors and ministers are expected to be silent
and non-controversial but, we pick up the broken lives that
our changing American culture is strewing across our land.
Lawmakers who are not in touch with reality, don't hear the
cries of despairing lives affected by policies that promote
freedom without accountability and responsibility. They are
actually creating problems that they later spend years debating
on how to fix and spend millions of dollars setting up commis-
sions to study how to recover the damage. Is that not insanity
gone wild?

I ask those who would want me to be silent,

"Have you held the hand of a dying Aids patient whom friends and families have abandoned? I have.

Have you looked for a family with four young children sleeping in the back of a truck on a rainy night to shelter them? I have.

Have you wiped the tears of a crying husband whose wife has chosen to abort their baby? I have.

Have you heard the deep silent sobs of broken-hearted young children when parents decide to go their separate ways? I have.

Have you given shelter to a broken abused woman who came to your door shivering in the cold night? I have.

Have you comforted young boys whose friend hanged himself in the schoolyard? I have.

Have you comforted parents whose beautiful only daughter was killed by a drunk driver? I have.

Have you heard the stories of people who have suffered from painful life-changing reverse discrimination? I have.

Have you sat across a man whose wife described him as perfect but boring, and ran off with another man, leaving him to take care of their young daughters? I have. He cried for 8 hours in my presence. I didn't know people had that much tears in their bodies?

Have you responded to a despairing call from a woman in the hospital who tried to take her own life by slitting her stomach because her lesbian lover left her for another woman? I have.

Have you sat in solitary confinement with a murderer who was seeking redemption and worrying about the family he left behind? I have.

Have you had to report a child to Child Protective Services because she was sexually attacking another girl? I have...only to find out that she had been forced to sleep with her grandmother's boyfriend who had had three children from his own daughter whom he had fathered with that grandmother. Complicated, sordid, and unfortunately true.

If you are too busy to notice our new normal, I hope you will take time to reflect on the state of your family, community, and our nation. And I want you to realize that it didn't happen by accident.

I think I have earned the right to speak out against the insane policies that are being passed without any thought to consequences or responsibilities...policies which are carving a painful and despairing culture we can hardly recognize.

But I speak out on behalf of thousands of ministers and pastors who, like me, do similar selfless unacknowledged acts every day. Some, like Mother Theresa, do it 24/7. We catch the broken and despairing human beings, the castaway problems that our insane policies have created. We hear their cries! We see the hopelessness in their eyes! Their desperate hands clutch ours as they silently beg for help. We are players on the field; we are not spectators in the stands nor Monday morning quarterbacks. What we increasingly see are the ravages of broken lives that are products of the insane, thoughtless, shortsighted, selfish policies of our country.

I speak as an American citizen. I have the right to free speech. I have my own opinions that have a right to be heard. I am speaking on behalf of the many unborn Americans who lost their right to life, liberty and the pursuit of happiness given by their Creator. I am speaking on behalf of people too broken or hurting to help themselves. I want some laws changed and others protected. I need the help of others who feel the same way.

Because the topics are pretty heavy and sometimes our eyesight too dim, I have tried to use my father's gift of humor to somehow help people see how insane we have become. If you object, please do not come to me with your arguments. Come and share with me your personal stories of fixing the brokenness of people in our beloved country who are not experiencing the American dream.

Since some of this contagious insanity seem to have begun in Hawaii, I felt perhaps, that I should do some investigating.

The more I researched, the more I realized that by letting insanity reign, we are doing a great injustice to the next generations. We must stop this fast-spreading infectious disorder. If we don't know where it came from, we will be like a dog trying to catch his tail.

Let's join the small Vigilant Patriots who have been warning us and praying for us to be awakened. Unless we realize that there has been a designed plot to destroy our righteous nation and be determined to fight back, vultures are ready to rule with their immorality. Our children are being victimized in the Divided States of America.

In my simple mind, the solution is easy: send the insane to Venezuela or Europe from where many of these ideas came, with a one-way ticket and soon they will be trying to get back as illegal aliens. Maybe that's why they don't want to build the wall.

The stupids who are intimidated by the insane should go back to their civics class. But alas, therein is the problem. According to an article in the NEA Today magazine entitled "Forgotten Purpose: Civics Education in Public Schools," they say that civic education is in crisis because only 25% of U.S. students are proficient in a civic assessment test. Ask them, "What do you know about Abraham Lincoln.

I think every elected government official should be given a civics test to qualify for candidacy. Maybe the field of those running for office would not be so crowded. I think they should at least be asked if they know the definition of the word "illegal."

Until 1960, the article says that American high school students had 3 basic civic courses. Over the years, they were slowly slashed and lost ground as the NCLB (no child left behind) era standardized the "Core Curriculum".

So, let's see where you stand. Remember, you can be a lawyer and qualify for the insane party. It's not what you know, but how you behave. If you don't know civics, you have automatic membership in the Stupid party. I hope you don't qualify for both.

Chapter Two

THE INSANE PARTY

(definition: not of sound mind; mentally deranged;
utterly senseless)

Test to qualify for the insane party
(vote "yes" or "no"; if you leave it blank, you automatically
qualify for the stupid party)

_____1. Everyone is his own moral authority. He should have the
right to do whatever he wants, whenever he wants, wherever he
wants. This is a free country. I believe in freedom!

_____2. I believe that if I work hard, I should be compassionate
and support my neighbor who doesn't have the urge to work. I
am for universal compassion.

_____3. I don't think I should build a fence or lock my door to
protect my family. That would be so unkind to the guy who

just came out of jail and needs a place to stay. I don't want to be judged as being prejudiced. I am against prejudice of any kind.

_____4. I am so glad they have restricted the sale of tobacco. It causes a lot of diseases and pollutes the air quality in enclosed areas. Marijuana is ok because it only leads to slight brain damage and it's your own brain, so it does not hurt others. It's the other more potent stuff it leads to that is so bad. I think it's wonderful that our youth can take it recreationally. They will have something that can take away their pain and make them happy. Cookies and candy are wonderful ways to let them sample Mary Jane. I wish they had recreational marijuana when I was younger. Plus, legalizing it will solve our problem of over-crowding prisons. The other prisoners could be more comfortable in prison. I am definitely for making people comfortable. In fact, if we pass more laws so we don't criminalize people, or strike down the ones that do, our overcrowded prison problem could be easily solved. I like solving problems.

_____5. It's okay to kill unborn babies. They don't know what is going on. Most are unwanted anyway and very inconvenient if you have a busy lifestyle. Looking at the parents, I think we are doing the world a favor. Human babies are beginning to be a growing threat to society. Some may grow up to be drug addicts, sexual predators, criminals, school shooters or insane politicians. I prefer saving the whales because they are an endangered species and they contribute so much to better the world. I am for positive contributions and preserving the species.

_____6. Graduate kids even if they can't read. If they can play a sport, great. They probably can get a scholarship to a famous university. In fact, everybody should have a free college education. It doesn't matter if you get a job or not after graduation. You can get a degree by taking courses like the physics of Star Trek from Santa Clara University or at Skidmore College: the sociology of Miley Cyrus. Have fun. Don't worry. The rich will be funding your fun! I am all for education. I am all for fun! I just can't figure out why so many with degrees are unemployed! It is baffling!!! I think I should go back to college to find out why. I would be in favor of the government funding my research in training these unemployed graduates to be legislators. I believe with their broad government subsidized education, they have ideas of how to solve some of these problems. They are our future so we should keep on investing in them. I like good investments!

_____7.   We should definitely ban all guns. Guns are very dangerous…especially as people get more brain damaged. We have a difficult time determining who is brain-damaged and we don't want to discriminate against those who are only slightly brain-damaged. So, to be fair and safe, we should ban all guns. Also, because we are smart enough to recognize that we can't stop criminals from having guns, we who are sane should set the example and not have guns. I am in favor of peace.

_____8. I have a right to choose my own gender. What do doctors know? People get confused when narrow-minded doctors decide what gender they are. The doctors know only two kinds. Let the unconfused child decide what gender it wants to be. There will be less confusion and more freedom in this country. I am definitely in favor of more freedom and less confusion!

_____9. All police are bullies so tell your kids they don't have to stop when the police command them to. Tell them if they get killed, you will be sure to blame the police on their behalf. You will hold parades in their honor, although the police may call them riots.

_____10. I believe we should channel angry women into a political force. I got some among my acquaintances. I always thought it was wasted energy and that it should be utilized for something. I oppose waste of any kind, especially energy. I love strong and angry women who are movers and shakers. I applauded when the female Speaker of The House wearing a lapel pin in the shape of the Mace, symbol of authority in the chambers recently tore up the President's State of The Union address. It was an awesome way to teach our young women how and when to be courageous. Wasted energy can be dressed in white and become very attractive. I like attractive, angry women! They spice up life!

_____11. I have been hurt or victimized so I will gather similar victims and riot. That's the only way to get things changed. Electing people who can change things takes too long. I notice that the loud and the violent get heard immediately. I like getting speedy attention!

_____12. If I cannot do well in men's sports, I have the right to change my sex so that I can be a champion in women's sports. I like winning trophies! Besides, the Russians were doing it illegally in the Olympics, I hear, so I love that it is legal here. I like being legal!

_____13. Masculinity is an illness and needs to be cured. I am glad our angry female politicians recognize that and are doing something to cure that! I like finding cures to incurable diseases!

_____14. We need to follow Minneapolis' brilliant idea to defund the police and replace policemen with a community-led public safety system. I think I will move to Minneapolis so I can really be safe.

If you voted "yes" to all these questions, congratulations! You are 100% insane!

You have unofficially joined thousands of college students who are taking courses like "Lady Gaga and the Sociology of Fame," which is taught at the University of South Carolina with a textbook from Amazon for $89. Other students are more intellectual and are taking at the University of California at Berkeley, "How to Argue with Judge Judy".

If you are ambitious enough, you may rise in the ranks of the insane party and run for office. This is the party to join because it seems like it's getting a lot of insane things done. You like getting things done fast!

In the past, the predecessors of this energetic and progressive party have worked very well across the aisle. They agreed to appropriate $398 million to construct a bridge to connect the town of Ketchikan, Alaska whose population was less than 9,000 to the airport on the Island of Gravina which had a population of 50. Although the insane Alaskan congressional delegation fought for it, smarter congressmen finally killed it. But it exposed the brilliance of insane legislators and the stupidity of our system.

If we had had some smart legislators, we in Hawaii could have used that generous funding. We need an inexpensive mode of intrastate transportation because we live in a very unique state consisting of 7 inhabited islands. It's not funny, but none of our local and national leaders, even the President, realize that the islands are surrounded by water and not connected to each other. I don't know where our interstate highway fund went but maybe the plans for a bridge from California to Hawaii are still on the drawing board.

Now the only way to get from island to island is by flying... on an airplane, that is. It recently cost me $400 roundtrip to go to another island for a funeral...a hundred-mile trip. In more ways than one, it would have been better if the funeral had been in Las Vegas, which we consider our 9th Island. A room, air and car deal could have been cheaper, and we could have cured our grief with some winnings and great buffets. We love buffets!

A very intelligent and compassionate governor got help to start a ferry system so we could take our cars to another island instead of having to rent one. But the insane who wanted to save the whales rather than human babies, fought and it died. It's amazing how cruise ships don't affect the whales. It could be that the cruise ships are bigger than the ferries and the whales could spot them better and avoid running into them. That's why we love to save them.

I discovered that they have a very cute name for projects like the Alaskan Bridge to Nowhere, as it was commonly called. For some reason, they wanted to honor the pig, so they called these, pork barrel deals. The pigs squealed in delight!

They kicked up their high heels and squealed again when they heard of the "Big Dig" in Boston. These progenitors of the Insane Party allocated nearly 15 billion...yes, billion dollars to re-locate a 3.5 mile stretch of highway underground. The work started in 1982 and finally ended in 2007. That was one way to help keep the unemployment rate low. Oh, but how it could have helped our wounded Veterans! Too bad there was nobody smart enough to think of that!

About that time, the stench of the pork in the barrels began to drift northward from Washington, D. C. to New York. A curious and perceptive man warily decided to see exactly from where the stench was coming. He found it to be drifting from a swamp in Washington, D.C.

He decided to throw his hat into the swamp to drain it. He didn't know at that time that there were a lot of crocodiles, alligators, snakes and vicious mermaids…oh, the mermaids, in the swamp, beside the barrels of rotting pork.

Being a man who liked challenges, he plunged in. With his noble intent, he didn't realize that the battle would be so intense. The only weapon he knew to use against the army of snakes and vicious mermaids, which the fake news was helping, was his tongue. When his tongue got tired, he tweeted.

He declared that he was going to Make America Great Again. He promised to Make America Safe Again, so he wanted to build a wall to keep the virus of globalism and chaos out. He wanted to Make America Prosperous Again and bring back American jobs that were given away to make other countries prosperous.

So, I ask every red-blooded and blue-blooded American, what's the beef? Why all this hatred toward him and these policies? He swears! He is very rough speaking! Have you done business with people from Queens, New York? I have! They all kinda speak like that! When I was offended, I was told that I had to talk like that with them to get things done. It worked

We have always complained that politicians never keep their campaign promises. Here is one who has.

He is busy getting righteous judges in our courts again, including the Supreme Court. He is helping preserve our religious liberties. If he doesn't get re-elected, we can very well be like Canada and some Scandinavian countries which are putting ministers in jail for, "hate speech," when we preach God's morality and God's standards.

I love men who keep their promises. No matter the personal flaws we all have, keeping your promise shows real character and your respect for those to whom you made those promises.

His courage has been stellar, and I don't know of anyone who could have withstood all the destructive forces that are intent to destroy him and our nation.

With all the squealing and the shaking, another party was exposed in this effort to control this country...the stupid! Surely the insane didn't think they could take over the country unless their opponent was stupid. Confusion was the best weapon and fake news was born. I resorted to Wikipedia to learn how stupid was different from the insane. I have come up with a test so if you flunked the previous test, take this next one.

Chapter Three

THE STUPID PARTY

(definition: lacking ordinary quickness and keenness of mind;
tediously dull, in a state of stupor)

"Whoever loves instruction loves knowledge,
but he who hates correction is stupid."
Proverbs 12:1

Test to Qualify For The Stupid Party
(before you take this test, I want to insincerely apologize if
the word stupid offends you. My mother said not to call anyone
stupid even if he is. I felt so guilty that I checked with Wikipedia
to see how many times "stupid" is mentioned in the Bible. It is
used 36 times so I know that God is smarter than my mother so
if it's ok with God, it should be okay with us. Relax!)

(vote "yes" or "no". You qualify for this party
if you answer all yes' or leave it blank)

_____1. I think our country is ok so I don't have to get involved.

_____2. I'm too busy. Let the politicians fight it out.

_____3. Que Sera, Sera (whatever will be, will be!) We can't change anything. Don't rock the boat! You know what is in the swamp.

_____4. I don't know too much about politics, and I don't like it so leave me alone.

_____5. Everyone has a right to his own opinion so why argue?

_____6. I'm too old. Let the young kids decide what they want. Remember, they can take courses like "How to debate with Judge Judy" at UC-Berkeley, so they should find something to argue about. Whether things change doesn't matter. Look at what's going on today!

_____7. I am religious and I don't want to get into anything dirty. It can really get dirty when you fall in the swamp.

_____8. Politics is so controversial; I don't want to get involved. I don't want to offend my friends. One thing I like about my friends…we don't mind being stupid together.

_____9. Politics is a calling for some, but not me. By the way, preachers should stick to their calling and not talk about politics.

_____10. My one vote won't matter so I will just pray that everything will turn out ok.

If you passed this test, you are now an official member of the Stupid Party and greatly responsible with what has happened to our country. The rest of the book is most definitely for you. Read on!

If you are feeling offended, it was the stupidity on the part of the National Association Of Evangelicals and the evangelical-supported Christianity Today Magazine which applauded the two Supreme Court decisions of 1962-63: the Engel V. Vitale and the Abington School District v. Schempp that ended prayer and Bible reading in the public schools.

Although the Rev. Billy Graham, Cardinal Francis Spellman and the liberal Episcopal Bishop James Pike decried these decisions, those representing evangelicals felt that the decisions appropriately separated the state from church affairs and that these practices had, anyway, become too secularized. Hence the great cultural wars we are now fighting with the generations which had no influence of God in their educational system. Have we repented of that stupidity? No God, no morality. Surprised that we are in this war?

This is why I am so passionate that we get educated. It is not our spirituality that will help us win; it is our stupidity that will sink us.

The cure for stupidity is education…the old-fashioned kind. The reason that insanity and stupidity are running amuck in our nation, is that we have long abandoned or forgotten the reason for our public school education. Our founding fathers wanted to be sure that future generations actively participate in our system of self-government.

Civic classes were designed to develop critical thinking, debating skills and strong civic virtues. It was meant for each generation to appreciate and preserve the God-given

Bible-based form of government which became the envy of the world. We should have been educated enough to be vigilant.

The unrest and anarchy in the 1960's began to open our eyes. We began to realize that the climate of our country had changed. People who opposed our form of government took advantage and worked hard to get their agenda realized while most of us were in a stupid stupor. Our curriculum had changed. Bible reading now was replaced by sex education. Prayer was replaced by psychological counseling after trauma. We made room for their agenda, remember?

The progressives in our country got busy and rewrote our history. One history textbook had several pages on Angela Davis and a short paragraph on Abraham Lincoln. I mention this just in case you are unaware of what has been happening. I hope it awakens parents to check their children's textbooks and perhaps run for the school board.

When we see our young people gravitating toward socialism, it makes my point because our young people do not know that Russia was the U.S.S.R. before it failed…The Union of Soviet Socialist Republics.

Do you know what form of government we have? The pledge of allegiance to the American flag gives a clue. Can you recite it?

> "I pledge allegiance to the flag of the United States of America, and to the Republic, for which it stands, one nation, under God, indivisible, with liberty, and justice for all."

This pledge is to the flag for which many young men and women died. When you disrespect it, you are cursing the ones who gave many the opportunity to go from poverty to riches in a few short years and kept them from risking their own lives for that privilege.

If you want to fight for injustice, use your money and run for office and make your point. That's how it's done in America. If angry destructive protests are done in the streets as our adversaries like George Soros want, we will no longer have a country where your children will be able to have the same privilege that you have been afforded.

It's amazing to me that the very system that allowed Americans like Bill Gates, and immigrants like Soros, to make more money than they can spend, is now being assaulted by those who successfully took advantage of it. To me, this is about as evil as human beings can get. If this is the pinnacle of human reasoning, we can die rich, but we will surely die miserable. To fan and support the riots that destroy America as George Soros unashamedly does, is the very depth of ingratitude, certainly not a very good legacy to leave behind.

We are a republic form of government, unique in that each citizen has a right to choose according to his own conscience. It was meant to be a very orderly, dignified, and cherished way to make changes in our government.

For review, here is a simple civics lesson. The Constitution of the United States of America sets up our Republic with three branches to create a balance of power.

1. The legislative branch: the branch that makes our national laws. It is comprised of
    A. The lower house: The House of Representatives with 435 voting members apportioned according to each state's population

    B. The upper house: the Senate which has two members from each state to ensure that both small and large states have equal power.

    C. We call these two bodies, the Congress of the United States of America. It can override presidential actions by a 2/3 vote of both houses.

2. The Judicial branch: the Supreme Court is the highest court in the Federal Judicial system. It has ultimate power over all federal and state court cases that involve a point of federal law. It can invalidate a statute for violating a provision of the U.S. Constitution. It can also strike down Presidential directives for violating either the Constitution or statutory law.

3. The executive branch consists of the President, Vice President and the Cabinet. The President is the Chief of State as he is the head of the government of the United States of America and Commander In Chief of the Armed Forces. The President can sign and enforce or veto any law congress passes. The Vice President stands ready to assume the presidency should the need arise. There are 15 executive departments, each headed by a person appointed by the President to form his Cabinet. These and several other federal agencies carry out the day to day responsibilities of the government under the President.

The ignorance of this is why so many don't vote or vote stupidly. They choose candidates on the basis of personality, looks, hair style, popularity, charisma, eloquence or the color of the skin.

Stupidity can be contagious. Look at your friends and see if you are catching it from them. You may have caught it at church because stupidity is no respecter of persons.

In the 1988 Presidential campaign, our stupidity caused one of the finest and smartest Godly men of our generation to lose because many Christians felt that a leader in the Christian community should not get involved in politics. His father had been a United States Senator, he had graduated from Yale with a law degree. Many knew him as a great man of God, a businessman who has successfully founded and has run the 700 Club until now. He is highly respected among world leaders.

If Christians had a chance to bring our country back to God, this was it. God, forgive us for our stupidity.

Half of the signers of our Declaration of Independence had divinity school training. As my mom would say, "It's ok to be stupid once. Learn from it and don't do it again." If we want our nation to survive, we need to have a President who fears God and surrounds himself with Godly people. I pray we will not be stupid again.

As we come out of our stupor, we realize don't we, that the strategy of the evil one has been to deceive us with lies and cause confusion in order to steal God's perfect plan for us.

I would like to audaciously add a fourth unauthorized and powerful branch of government: the media.

Initially, the simple media reported the activities of their communities and, in the larger sense, reported the doings of elected officials as they saw it. It informed the common citizen as to how their government was progressing. That was fine, until moral authority was removed and there was no accountability. Character was not important. But, making a reputation and money for oneself became acceptable.

Other forms of media added to the moral decay. Under the guise of free speech, relentless attacks on families, emasculating men, oversaturation of sex and violence, sensationalizing of selected events for their purposes have been a major cause of our shameful state of being.

The arrogance of these self-appointed demagogues and others like them, has taken our moral values and politicized them so that they can change the basic values of our country. To me the most frightening are these who are not elected by the people, having no accountability, audaciously define our values. The defense of our long-held values is then labeled by them as "hate speech."

They have made what they consider, "politically correct," to be the standard for all and discount our desire to be "morally correct." When they call me a bigot or homophobic, I call that hate speech. This travesty of freedom could never happen if moral people stood up and said something. We had better toughen up and get ready to fight back when they label us with hate-evoking terms. I see it already in some of the research I have done: fringe conspiracy theorists, religious zealots, religious fundamentalists, alarmists, etc.

Know what they are trying to do and be proud of their opinion of you. They are fighting what you stand for, not you necessarily.

I believe we should be allowed to express our deepest convictions with respect for the person. Surely even the worst of us have some sense of right or wrong. We may not agree, but the first amendment guarantees our right of free speech.

When our freedom robs another of their life, liberty and pursuit of happiness, I believe we have mocked this freedom. With no boundaries and decency, fake news has ruined lives of celebrities who don't have the freedom to enjoy some measure of privacy and respect. Tabloids are the best examples.

I think the news media learned well from them that we can doctor photographs, soundbytes, sensationalize a shadow and sell it for a good price. It also gives them higher ratings. In order to be first to report things, they have almost become prophetic. They project and build a story and then fill in details they hope will be true as they race to get it out first. They will take soundbytes and use pictures and use them for their profit.

I think we all suspected for years that the news was becoming more slanted to reflect the reporter's or network's bias. I saw it firsthand at the 1988 Republican party convention in New Orleans. One of the nation's top Nightly News reporters almost couldn't come down from his news tower at the end of the night. He had reported that the young college volunteers were being paid well and were put up in fancy hotels. They were in fact staying in college dorms.

Because people are aware of this media war, I sense that many have become disinterested. So, I believe the media sensationalizes events so they can have a good rating. I believe that those who are informed and have a platform, should speak out. It is our opportunity to lead people back to the great America we all so desire.

When we see the enormous power of the media infiltrating all three of the established branches of government, we need to remember that in a Republic, we are the most important factor. We have the power to vote for someone who will represent our views and we have still the freedom to speak up.

Look up David Barton's Wall Builders website, www. wallbuilders.com. Instead of getting your fake civic lessons from schools and fake news, get real facts from Barton's life-long research and documentation of America's unique

Judeo-Christian heritage. Let's turn back the wicked, "Cancel Culture" movement. Get educated and vote only for candidates who truly know the history of our country and love it.

If we don't vote, we are saying to the many young soldiers who made the ultimate sacrifice to give us the right to vote, "Your death to keep me free and empower me to vote, means nothing." If you are black and don't vote, you are saying to your forefathers who were demeaned as slaves and not given the right to vote, "Your fight for the right to vote means nothing."

We have an obligation as citizens in this free country to learn the issues that are at stake and seek the politicians who hold our values or should get informed and consider running for office. We need to consider what kind of country we are going to leave to the next generation.

Because the fight for the soul of our country is the battle of the Godly versus the ungodly, the main question to ask is their position on the right of the unborn child to live. This will indicate whether they want expediency over morality.

I hope we aren't stupid again. We have caused a lot of good candidates to lose because of our ignorance. I hope you will learn through this book that there are people and organizations that have long set out to destroy our Godly nation. Search your heart and have a plan to make our country a place you will be happy to leave to your children and grandchildren. Recent generations have been more preoccupied trying to satisfy themselves than provide a better future for their children.

We must be determined not to lose this present Civil War. Much is at stake and if you wonder what it will be like if we lose, catch up on the news from Venezuela. We very well could be another Venezuela within five years.

Do you think that all this insanity and stupidity just sprang up one night when we were sleeping?

Only after I started researching for this project did I learn how long and well planned this revolution has been. The material that I will share now is from a documentary put out by the Catholic church on their T.V. channel EWTN: "A Wolf in Sheep's Clothing." It was directed by Stephen Payne, and produced by him, Richard Payne and C.F. Miller. Eternal word T.V. network presented it and it was the production of Arcadia Films, Ltd.

If you and your friends passed the stupid test, throw "a wolf in sheep's clothing party." You can get it from ewtnrc.com or call 1-800-854-6316. If it doesn't get you good and mad, you can stay stupid! It tells how insanity infiltrated the Catholic Church and offers a solution to Catholics.

The Catholics are telling their story here, but in the early 1900's, liberal Protestant theologians and social activists infiltrated the Protestant denominations. They set up the National Council of Churches in 1950. These denominations are now warring over the issues of abortion and gay marriages. They are using the same tactics, same divisive agenda to accomplish their goals to change our Godly society into a godless one. Socialistic progressive ideas invaded our churches. This powerful Catholic documentary introduced me to the power of one!

Chapter Four

THE P O W E R OF ONE: SAUL ALINSKY (1909-1972)

Don't forget his name!!!

H e was admired and studied by Hillary Rodham Clinton. She wrote a 92-page senior thesis for Wellesley College entitled, "There's Only the Fight…An Analysis of The Alinsky Model." Would it be surprising to you that Matt Patterson of the Washington Post, reported that, "Obama received a comprehensive course in Saul Alinsky during his years as a community organizer in Chicago, an experience Obama recalled as 'the best education he ever had."

Charles Krauthammer wrote in 2017, "The Enemy Amongst Us!!" An October 11, 2017 article from the New York Post, revealed former President Obama's organization called "Organized for Action." It is modeled after what he learned from Saul Alinsky about community organizing.

At present, there are about thirty thousand members working to disrupt what the current administration is doing. He and his wife and former administration leaders are directing, what Paul Sperry from the New York Post said is a shadow government to sabotage the Trump administration's agenda. Through a network of non-profits led by OFA, it has a war chest of more than forty million dollars and 250 offices nationwide. Check their website to get more information. Watch the news to observe the speedy and radical actions against our President's programs.

In addition, Patterson reports that "he was schooled by disciples of Alinsky himself, including Mike Kruglik, who remembered Obama as "the best student he ever had, a natural... undisputed master of agitation."

I don't think that even loyal Democrats know that, so you will learn why our nation is so on fire with hate and agitation.

Even the casual observer of Alinsky's teachings know that his simple evil plan was to generate conflict to mobilize the dispossessed.

So, please, allow me to introduce you to the man and his progressive aggressive cohorts who want to run our country with hate and violence. Once you know a little about him and others who are willing to fund his dream, you will understand what is going on.

Alinsky was born in 1909. He had a bitter distant relationship with his father but was attached to his overbearing mother. He was brought up in an orthodox Jewish home.

He is described as a

20th century rebel
Father of community organizing
Pet revolutionary of the Church People of America
Organizer of the poor

(desired for the poor to rise up and reject middle-class values)
Self-proclaimed agnostic and socialist
New Left Radical
During the Depression, he aligned with the new Left-wing
    liberal group in the Democratic party
Allied with Frank Netti, successor of Al Capone,
Allied with Herb March, member of the Young Communists
Launched a political force, The New Democracy
He worked with the National Catholic Youth Organization

At the University of Chicago, taking up sociology and crim-
inology, he had a desire to change the inner cities of America.
He described his community organizing in his book "Reveille
for Radicals."

It is filled with the amorality found in Europe's Marxists
battlefields. His philosophy was that "Noble goals should be
pursued by any means." His community organizing groups
learned to unite disenfranchised people by seeking their hurts
and needs, working together on small projects that were easy
to do, fully gain their confidence and then empower them to
fight for changes. Because morality was not an issue, they were
taught to accomplish their goals by any means necessary.

Bella Dodd, a former ranking communist, in 1944, deliv-
ered a speech at Fordham University. She had returned to her
Catholic faith and revealed that in the 1930's, the Communists
put men in the Catholic Church. She said that these men now
were rising in the power structure of the church. Alinsky had
used the community organizing tactic to get these vulnerable
priests who were assigned to do the social welfare work of the
Church. He used their influence to foment rebellion against the
ecclesiastical order of the Church.

Cardinal Kroll warned that radicals were trying to take over as the National Call to Action Conference was being held in Detroit in 1976. Archbishop Bernadin, President of the Bishop's Conference and Monsignor Egan, board member of Alinsky's Industrial Areas Foundation were co-chair of the Conference.

On the Protestant side, look up the ministry of the Reverend Jeremiah Wright, Jr. He led the congregation of Trinity United Church of Christ in Chicago for 36 years. He studied black liberation theology. He was influenced by Dr. James H. Cone, a theologian best known for his advocacy of black liberation theology. His 1969 book "Black Theology and Black Power" defined black power as black people asserting the humanity that white supremacy denied.

If you were not totally sleeping recently, you will remember a "community organizer" from Chicago, born in Hawaii became president after not serving a full term in the U.S. Senate. Does that ring a bell? He and his wife were married by Dr. Wright and their children were baptized by him. But they dropped their long membership there when the sermons Dr. Wright was preaching, exposed his extreme views against America.

It shouldn't be strange to you now that while he was President there was rising racial violence and anti-police riots.

It shouldn't be strange to you that under Hillary Clinton's run for office, angry women rose up to run this country.

So, under the radar and with attractive innocuous sounding names, a godless humanism invaded our pulpits and infected our people.

Alinsky agreed with Norman Thomas, America's socialist Presidential candidate in the 1940's who said that the American people will never adopt socialism. But, under the name Liberalism and Progressivism, America will become a socialist nation without knowing how it happened.

How surprised they would be that in the Presidential race in 2020, there would be a Socialist candidate who is not hiding behind nice names. The old candidate is proud to be a Socialist and thrilled that so many young people are following him. It is so even in the light of current news that socialist Venezuela is in chaos and people are starving. Venezuela which had been one of the richest of South American countries with vast natural resources is a mess! Isn't that insanity?

Maybe they realize that the rest of us would not be so stupid to accept an outright socialist. So, what are they offering? Obama's partner, an embarrassment but easily manipulated to carry out their agenda.

Are you awake yet? Do you realize that unless we rise-up and do something, the battle will be lost? Do you need another bell?

In 1971, Alinsky wrote the book, "Rules for Radicals". He dedicated this book to Lucifer, "The First Radical Who Was Very Effective."

Alinsky followed Karl Marx's "conflict theory: the life of man on earth is a warfare." Wonder why all the divisive conflicts? Wonder how our basic moral rights and values were politicized so we could fight about them? Even the recent Coronavirus outbreak quickly became a political issue so we could argue about it, instead of solving the crisis.

He chose to follow Marx's choice for the afterlife, too. One of Marx's poetry said:

"I wish to avenge myself against the one who rules above...... I will wander god-like and victorious through the ruins of the world.

Heaven is forfeited. I know it full well, my soul once true to God is chosen for hell."

A few weeks before Alinsky died in 1979, he told the interviewer from Playboy Magazine:

> "if there is an afterlife and I have anything to do
> with it, I will unreservedly choose to go to hell.
> Hell would be heaven to me. Once I get into
> hell, I will start organizing the have-nots...with
> a smile. They are my kind of people."

He lived off the wealth of two rich wives and dropped dead on a sidewalk with a massive heart attack, after visiting one of them.

Thus, ends the life of Saul Alinsky. But the seeds of the immoral insanity he planted during his rather short life are in full bloom. The horrific statistics of our broken, divided nation full of conflicts, are the evidence. He took his trophies to hell and celebrated with Lucifer. However, his disciples have carried on:

Max Horkheimer and Theodore Adorno developed "Political correctness."

Gyorgky Lukecs, Eric Fromm, Wilhem Reich and Herbert Marcuse used Sigmund

Freud's "Pan-Sexualism: The Search for Pleasure" and Michael Walsh's "The Devil's Palace" to start the sexual revolution. They explored the difference between the sexes to incite gender conflict. They also explored their commonalities to incite gender confusion which is in exponential growth at present.

The plan was to overthrow from within begin by changing family life. See if they haven't infiltrated our:

media
education
law

military
entertainment
unions
churches
sports
and other groups to succeed in their efforts to change
our nation!

Look at what has happened to the Boy Scouts of America!
Did you ever think......??? This is the cross pollination of
insanity and stupidity.

Awake yet??? Throw your "Wolf in Sheep's Clothing" party
and wake up from your nightmare.

Alinsky learned his strategy from Fabius Maximus, a
Roman General:

1. Win by patience and attrition
2. Avoid open confrontation
3. Slowly dumb-down and change moral standards of
   your enemies.

If you realize that the insanity, we are now experiencing was
a well-planned and executed one, do you see yourself as one of
his trophies?

I hope you are good and mad at Insanity and Stupidity. I
hope you will stand with the Crazy Courageous and fight back.
Let's go back to the basics...see what we lost and how we can
get our beloved America back. We lost because we didn't fight.
Let's fight back!

Chapter Five

WHAT DID THE ENEMY STEAL FROM US?

I n this pathetic Civil War, two sides are angry and glaring at each other. Frustrated and desperate, but, without common morality, there will not be a common resolution. Both are determined to win, one very fiercely.

For those of us who are just realizing how serious this Civil War is, we are sensing what we have lost. We have to be humble enough to admit that our complacency, our contentment, our stupidity has caused all this destruction. I hope we will be courageous enough to get involved and commit ourselves to restoring what the enemy stole from us.

Tom Brokaw, former NBC news anchor and author, wrote a book entitled, "The Greatest Generation," referring to those who were born just before the great depression and who came of age in World War II.

Personally, I am grateful that my grandparents made the courageous decision to leave their homeland and come to seek a better life for their families. My grandparents had emigrated from Okinawa, Japan, at the turn of the 20th century. My maternal grandparents made enough money to return to Okinawa to escape the Great Depression in America. My paternal grandparents bought a small pineapple farm and were quite self-sufficient living off the land, so they were not affected much by the depression.

Accounts of long unemployment lines and bread lines became common scenarios in large cities. Horrific stories of the many rich who committed suicide as they lost their fortunes added to the emotional despair and depression. Europe was seething with unrest.

My grandfathers were too young for World War I and too old for the second World War. But their sons joined millions of others to defend and protect our nation when Japan audaciously attacked Pearl Harbor (for civics students, that drew the USA into the second World War). It left Japanese Americans in a very difficult situation. Those from the West Coast and some from Hawaii had property, bank accounts and other possessions seized by The United States government within a few days. These were never returned.

My father who returned as a decorated soldier said that the only good that came out of that horrible war, personally, is that he became a born-again Christian.

Likewise, for those who had been taken to concentration camps, many had become Christians. A few college students who had become Christians before the war, spread the good news of Jesus in those camps. Because of their new-found faith, one father could say to his children, "Despite what we went through, America is still the best country in the world."

His daughter, my friend, Michi Tanioka helped edit a book, "Triumphs of Faith: Stories of Japanese-American Christians

During World War!!" It recorded the testimony of her own family, too. After the war, many went to Japan and other places around the world where Japanese had settled and spread the good news they had found in Jesus.

As they were released to fend on their own, many churches helped them. Their newfound trust in God helped them move forward without bitterness. Within a few years, with the favor of God, many became millionaires as they channeled their energies into hard work. I am proud of this and I think this is the example we need to follow in these times of racial tensions and injustices.

That terrible war, however, changed our American culture. We lost our traditional families. As men went to war, women manned the factories. They gained the taste for financial independence and power.

Alinsky's theory of divide and conquer, pitting the sexes against each other was seeded and has come full bloom.

With father and mother divided, children rose up to power. They set the agenda, the fashion, the culture not only for their family, but for the nation.

To the delight of those whose strategy was to incite hatred and riots, they sat back and paid these restless, wasted ones with the finances they were able to acquire in our great entrepreneurial country.

Sadly, what we didn't realize was that the breakdown of our families would lead to the breakdown of our American way of life. There was no one to teach our children simple moral values. Plus, there were these vultures waiting for the opportunity to indoctrinate them, teaching them that they were free thinkers and could do anything they wanted. Situation ethics became a cool way to live for those already lost in deception.

Sadly too, is that we lost our civility as a nation. We don't respect our national symbols and treasures. We don't respect our institutions. This is the "Cancel Culture Movement," that is part of our enemies' plan. They want us to destroy our past so they can build a new America. Remember the Marxist plan for a one world domination?

We don't respect each other. We simply don't have good manners anymore. I don't think our young people know what that means. It certainly is not being modeled for them. I remember when female reporters demanded to be admitted to the locker rooms after a long hard-fought football game. The guys wanted to shower and just hang out. How rude! Women would call the men perverts if they demanded the same. I was disgusted.

The drama of the Brett Kavanaugh confirmation hearings illustrated how far our society has spiraled downward. As a woman, I was deeply saddened. Something killed our nurturing gifts because of the spirit of death we allowed through abortion. We have been robbed of the joy and pleasure our maternal giftings provided. Our families depended on us for emotional stability. Women had the natural instinct of bringing peace and reconciliation and hence, comfort, to the family. We saw the opposite at the hearings.

The educated women who represented their States on that Judicial Committee, used the sacred halls of our government to showcase their anger. What I saw played out was the Alinsky theory of victimization and anger in order to enflame and cause riots, their selected method to bring change. Can we hate so deeply that we would make fools of ourselves as we destroy lives?

As soon as I saw the "Star" showcased in the courtroom meekly, weakly answer questions, my female instincts sensed drama.

As though I needed it confirmed, late one-night I found my T.V. on C-SPAN2, which I very seldom watch. I thought it strange, so I sat and watched what was on. I could not believe the discussion and could not believe that it was being played out during the Kavanaugh hearings. It was like the script for the hearings. What I heard was what I was seeing on the Nightly News.

It was an interview of Rebecca Traister and the review of her book: "Good and Mad, The Revolutionary Power Of Women's Anger." She is a writer for New York magazine and she was being interviewed by Britney Cooper, Rutgers University women's and gender studies Professor and author of "Eloquent Rage." What a team, laughing and enjoying their brilliance.

Alinsky would be so proud. The script was well-written and the drama spellbinding. He must have applauded in hell for the terrific performance.

What is with these female professors? Have they become so intelligent that they have somehow discovered a behavioral example of where anger triumphs over peace and hate triumphs over love? What are they celebrating?

Have they so long been out of touch that they don't realize that in a family, we used to teach our children not to resort to violence when they disagreed, not to use bad words, not to steal, not to lie and cheat and we required them to do some chores? Why do they think that doing the opposite will be for the good of all?

You know what? People who haven't been to college or gotten as much education as they have, must be glad, because the intelligence displayed by those two looked insane to me.

I am very proud of the battered women whom I have befriended and am helping at this time. I commend them for not choosing to be used by movements that would victimize them further. They have the courage to take the hard road of healing and restoration so that they, by example, can lead their children out of the environment of anger and violence and give them a better life.

Through them, we have seen love conquer hate, and peace replace violence. You are trophies, you courageous women! You are setting a great example for your next generation and for our nation.

I think most can now see through the 'Me Too" movement. All the scantily clad women who followed men to their hotel rooms or other secluded places, should apologize for baiting the men; and all the men who took the bait and abused them should apologize to them.

One good thing about America, we try to be fair and look at both sides.

Those who ruined Harvey Weinstein's reputation knowing he was married, should apologize to his wife and his family; and he should apologize to all those he abused when he didn't get their permission. Harvey, the courts said you deserve jail time but I know your greater pain is the abandonment by your children. I hope your children will forgive you. Maybe when they get older, they will realize that it is very difficult to live in a world when nobody respects a wedding ring anymore...especially if it is on a rich man's finger.

Forgiveness is a great gift you can give away with no regrets. I hope your children can do that. The lesson on forgiveness is what America needs to learn today if we are to be great again. But where is that black book which demonstrated what forgiveness is?

Hear ye! Hear ye! Wake up! Did you know that that sacred black book has been replaced by the sacred writings of the mighty Saul Alinsky? Remember, his disciples like Hillary

Clinton and Chicago's former Mayor, Ron Emmanuel have been heard saying, "Never waste a crisis". They embrace the Marxist idea that every thesis has an antithesis and will eventually produce a synthesis…of confusion and hate!

Repeatedly we see them taking the thesis of a God-ordained plan for us and create an antithesis for us to battle over, to come up with a synthesis they have pre-selected.

There has been a plot to destroy our families by first destroying you men. It's all revealed in a great timely book, "Man to Man: Rediscovering Masculinity in A Challenging World."

No wonder the title! The author is three-star Lt. General (ret.) William Jerry Boykin, original member of the Delta Force and one of the leaders of the Green Berets.

In the 1950's, there was a popular show, "Father Knows Best." It portrayed dad as the wise, stable guy always taking challenging situations and coming up with a solution. This was like a typical American family.

In 1958, as reported in General Boykin's book, The Communist Party of the USA released its book, "The Naked Communist," which laid up plans to take over America. Because families are the foundation of any nation, they set forth to destroy our families, beginning by taking down the men.

They worked it hard through the media, entertainment, politics and our education system. They have taught classes on, "Toxic Masculinity." There has been an epidemic of pornography, gender confusion and homosexuality. We cannot forget the fun wife-swapping parties that became acceptable.

Has Alinsky and his cohorts succeeded? What do you think?

Ah, but wait! I hear the clarion call of that courageous Delta Force general to join him and put up a fight. Get his book! Watch him on YouTube. Be inspired to be courageous. And there are others like him. Thank God!!!

We need to get back to God's instruction book for families. We need to rebuild what Satan has tried to tear down.

Satan has intimidated us by accusing that Godly men are tyrants and women are passively submissive slaves. Toughen up and get used to their "toxic" name calling. This is how they have silenced us before.

We have many visible families and leaders in our Christian community who are displaying the orderly, successful plan of a God who knew how to design families. Be determined to make your family an example in your community. It was His idea in the first place so be courageous because you cannot fail.

When I saw General Boykin interviewed on the 700 Club, I knew God was giving us another chance.

I say, rise up, o men of God. When you are strong and love us as Christ loves the church, we ladies, feel protected, secure, and proud. We will follow, honor, and support you. God's way is so very simple if we don't care who gets the credit!!!

Chapter Six

WHO SOUNDED
THE TRUMP-ET?

When I learned that the godless had decided that masculinity was a toxic disease, it confirmed my suspicions. When we become our own God: insanity and stupidity set in. As you know, I feel that stupidity can be cured. Proverbs 12:1 says that if you hate correction you are stupid, so I figure that if you love correction you can be cured of stupidity.

The American Psychological Association feels that masculinity is a very serious illness. Ryon Mcdermott, a psychologist who helped the APA find a cure says that he found in comparing men with women, the recession hit men harder than women, they are less likely to graduate from college, and men are more likely to complete suicide.

Hmmmm…I wonder about the cause of this awful disease! I think it's smarter first to find the cause and then the cure.

Let me think for half a second. Could it be mental abuse, since these geniuses think it is a psychological disease?

Could the constant barrage over a generation that told men that they were bigots, stupid, clumsy, out of touch, failures, inferior to women, depraved sexual predators, good for nothings, be the cause?

Is that why the insane are so against the Second Amendment rights? It definitely represents the disease of masculinity! Yes, take away gun rights and you will cure the disease of masculinity. Look around! There are a lot of examples of males who have been cured of masculinity.

Did I figure that out all by myself or should I return to college and get another degree to confirm how brilliant I was to figure it out on my own?

No wonder the godless hide their Presidential candidate in the basement. I think they suspect he may have that disease so he must appear that he doesn't. They are succeeding with their strategy.

Plus, give me another half a second. They will cover it up by choosing a person who definitely doesn't have that disease...a real, no sex-change or added hormones woman to be his running mate. Off in the wings, are those white-clad women who will use their stored-up power of anger to rule him and our nation. They will be celebrating getting rid of that awful disease called masculinity!!!

Why do you think our President's term of office has been so attacked and disrupted. It is because women don't like to lose. If we do, we cry, whine, pout and continue the argument until we feel like we win… and make everybody miserable. You've seen the sign: "if momma ain't happy, nobody's happy." When real men lose, they suck it up and move on.

No wonder they hate President Trump

They are afraid of him because he has a very bad case of this horrible disease…masculinity. It seems like his is incurable. I am sure they don't want Joe Biden to be on stage debating him because of fear that it may be contagious. Even the warmongering leader of North Korea, I hear, prefers to be seated when they are interviewed or pictured together. He doesn't want to have to look up to him, looking like a shrimp or looking feminine.

Know why women support our President? We have the disease of femininity and we feel very safe with men who are affected with masculinity...the God-given kind. I don't like his language at times, but when there is danger lurking, I would rather have a Pitbull than a French Poodle guarding me. You notice that when there is a threat by a foreign entity, he stands strong, draws the line and responds quickly in the strongest language with a stronger threat. (I like his scowl) then, he consults his staff...which makes politicians uneasy. I am sure he knows his limitations, but it keeps the enemy guessing. Just not knowing if he is crazy or not, keeps the enemy at bay...a good strategy, I think.

A financial giant, he wants to make America great again because he wants each American to live his American dream by working for it himself. He wants you to keep your hard-earned wages and not let the government take it and put it in a pork barrel. He wants those with entrepreneurial gifts to keep expanding and providing jobs for everyone.

With our economy as it is now, it should be a no-brainer to have the most well-known successful entrepreneur at the helm. But, of course, the no-brainers will have to be convinced and because insanity seems to be incurable, we definitely will have a challenge.

Do I see him as perfect? I don't want to cast the first stone in case Jesus is watching.

Since I was once on the Rules committee of The National Republican Party when Pat Robertson was running, I think, I have been getting questionnaires from time to time about my opinion as to how I think the President is doing. These have been my answers, some of which were forwarded directly to his email.

1. Learn good behavior from your children.
2. Your impulsive demeaning comments do not dignify your office.
3. Read the second half of Daniel chapter 4 and remember Nebuchadnezzar when you lie on your bed and think how wonderful you are. Before honor is humility.
4. If you shut your mouth, you can win re-election hands down.
5. Responses or reactions to trivial impromptu situations do not need a tweet. If you keep quiet, you will hear your opponents self-destructing.
6. Let others brag about your accomplishments. Self-adulation is very unattractive. Thank God for your beautiful, dignified wife who makes it easier to appreciate you. If she can love you, you must not be too bad. I heard that you are very kind and nice in person.

On the other hand, I do acknowledge my appreciation for his using his audacious personality to stand against the insanity that is going on in our country. I guess I can't have my cake and eat it, too. I think his unpredictable fearlessness is what is cleaning out the Swamp and making other countries respect us again.

I voted for him the last time because the other candidate had swum in the long Swamp from Chicago by way of Arkansas, to Washington D.C. and was pretty stinky by the time she arrived. I voted for him that first time mainly because he promised to work for issues that are extremely important to me.

In fact, I felt so strongly about the issues, I went out, sometimes alone, in central Maui to hold campaign signs for him (I was crazy then, too). The biggest reason I am voting for him now is that he has kept his promises, unlike most politicians.

His past record gives me confidence that he will continue to make America great again and respected by the world.
I want to thank him for:

1. His strong pro-life stand. How can we vote for someone who is willing to kill a baby, our most precious natural resource? How can anyone with a conscience look into the peaceful face of an infant and consider killing him? We didn't get this barbaric overnight, but slowly our senses were numbed (like Alinsky planned) until we are able to kill a baby outside the womb...and celebrate!
2. His careful preparation and choices for Supreme Court Justices and other judges. This ranks very close to the top of my priority list. The winner of the next election will probably appoint two or three lifetime judges on the Supreme Court. If you love your grandchildren, this is the issue you should most carefully consider. These justices will set the course for America for the next half a century, at least. I foresee that if he doesn't win, we pastors will go through intense persecution if we preach as we should, and our freedom of religion and speech will be lost. What we believe as the moral conscience of God, is considered hate speech by the other side.
3. His quiet work to insure and protect our religious liberties is huge.
4. His ability to get deals negotiated and done is genius. His brashness keeps world leaders guessing and he uses that for our advantage. As I travel to other countries, the respect for our nation is returning. Getting other member nations to pay their fair share doesn't make them dislike us. It lets them know that we are not stupid and they respect us for that. This is one area I

believe America is becoming great again, even if many Americans don't appreciate it.

5. His support for our military and our defense is commendable. The priority in this area should be to take care of military families and returning soldiers, especially if they are wounded. We cannot honor them in parades and then leave them destitute. If we can find money in the pork barrels to fund ridiculous bridges and unnecessary highways, we can find money to provide resources for a comfortable life for our heroes. After all, they are the ones who are sacrificing and making it possible for us to accomplish our American dream. It's a disgrace, especially for the wounded, that their standard of living is below ours.

6. His revival of our Space program. Somewhere along the way, somebody insane decided that we didn't need to lead in this area. If we don't, we leave ourselves unprotected, vulnerable and obsolete.

7. What he has done for Israel is courageous and historic. Ever since my mother became a Christian, she has loved Israel and taught us to love Israel, too. We have visited Israel several times. Just before her death, we learned that she had been using her social security checks every month, to bring elderly Russian Jews back to Israel. On election night, I was in Israel and I went to bed thinking Trump had lost the election. I woke up to find out that a miracle had taken place. My Israeli friend gave me the newspaper at breakfast which reported his unexpected victory. I think I laughed for five minutes. I told my friend that I knew now that our embassy would be moved from Tel Aviv to Jerusalem. His wry reply was that all recent Presidents had also promised and not come through and

that he didn't expect that it would happen. Our President's boldness accomplishes what others only promise to do. I was again in Israel when it was announced that he was indeed going to move the embassy to Jerusalem, and the next month, he did. I believe that he and our nation are blessed because he has blessed Israel. During this tumultuous term of office, despite the sore losers on the other side, he has secured the Golan Heights and Jerusalem for Israel. Now, he is boldly adding Judea (where Bethlehem is) and Samaria, by his supportive proclamations. It is amazing that some of his opponents have Jewish roots and do not support the nation of Israel...the only democracy and true friend we have in the area.

8. He will not surrender to globalism. The reason he is hated by politicians in both parties is because this idea is embraced by both. I was invited to the Inauguration of President George H. W. Bush because I had been a delegate to the Convention which had nominated him. The night before the Inauguration, sitting with others at the Lincoln Memorial, we witnessed a magnificent ceremony as both the president's and the vice president's families were introduced. I remember his speech about a Thousand Points of Lights which I didn't quite understand. What I suddenly picked up was the mention of a One World Order. I had goose bumps. Oddly enough, returning from the Inauguration, I noticed for the first time the logo on the American Airlines plane... member of the One World Alliance. It was creepy. At present, there are thirteen airlines that are members. When I returned to Jerusalem a few months later, my friend took me to a War Memorial overlooking the Jordan valley. He told me that the new President had

just withdrawn U.S. funds from building protective settlements on that border. Countries that move toward globalism will always be against Israel. That's why the Swamp with bi-partisan opposition in some instances, despise him. Did we ever think that there would be a day when Americans would not want to be great, and choose, rather, to be like other countries? That is about as unamerican as can be and it is frightening!

9. In his book, "God and Country: The Christian Case for Trump", Ralph Reed, devotes thirty pages, listing all the accomplishments of President Trump, especially strengthening our religious liberties. Dr. Reed started the Christian Coalition and is the founder of the Faith and Freedom Foundation. His website will keep you updated.

10. Even as I am writing this, I get this announcement from President Trump's network. He is calling for a National Day of Prayer for the on-going crisis of this coronavirus:

"It is my great honor to declare Sunday, March 15th as a National Day of Prayer. We are a country that, throughout our history, has looked to God for protection and strength in times like these. No matter where you may be, I encourage you to turn towards prayer in an act of faith. Together we will easily prevail."

Note: the last President cancelled the traditional National Day of Prayer event at the White House but fifty thousand Muslims gathered on the steps of the Capitol to have a day of prayer.

He is not perfect. We are not electing a priest. He is our Commander in Chief and we need one who can fight against the insanity overtaking our country. I am glad that he will represent me and fight for my values in this vicious Civil War. Our precious vote is our weapon and, if you can convince five others, you can be considered a warrior!

I don't believe he is our President by accident. There is a Bible in his Oval Office which is the reason why. God who is faithful to hear fervent prayers, heard the prayers of two old sisters in the Hebrides Islands, off the coast of Scotland.

They were in their 80's; one was blind and other bent over so they could not go to church. However, they opened their home to prayer meetings asking God for a revival.

Rev. Duncan Campbell responded, and a great revival did break out. A young man, Donald Smith fervently helped the preacher. He was the nephew of these two ladies. Their niece, his cousin, emigrated to the United States. Her name was Mary Ann Smith McCloud who married a businessman named Fred Trump in New York.

A Bible was sent to her from that revival. Mary Ann named her second son after her cousin Donald and gave him that Bible. Donald Trump, our 45th President, has the Bible of his grandaunts' revival in the Oval Office. I can't help but believe that the prayers of his grandaunts are being honored and God is pleased.

Ah, God-fearing ones, this is the movement we have been waiting for!

> "How could one man chase a thousand, and two
> put ten thousand to flight……?"
> Deuteronomy 32:30

Let's flutter our wings and follow our Crazy Courageous leader and have a hurricane victory!!!

Chapter Seven

THE POWER OF TWO... GOD AND YOU

**IF GOD
BE FOR YOU
WHO CAN
BE
AGAINST
YOU?**

In these scary uncertain times, do you know that you need God and God needs you?

Our relationship with our Creator God means more than life itself. His Eternal Word, the Bible, has the plan for this earth and all its inhabitants. There was a beginning and there will be an end. The Bible has been proven to give an accurate account of earth's past, and because of that, we can be sure that what it says about the future will come to pass.

The Bible was written by about 40 holy men, inspired by God's Holy Spirit, living on three continents, over a period of about 1,500 years. Its message is singular: Creator God loves us. When we turn away from Him, we bring disaster upon ourselves. When we humble ourselves and turn to Him, He rescues us.

Because He is a God of order and absolutely fair, He who said that every sin committed earns death, came Himself to absolve us by dying on the Cross for us. That was a demonstration of His infinite love. In other words, He paid the debt of our wages of sin so through Him we legally can live forever in heaven where our Father is waiting for us.

From His holy perspective, He sees us all as sinners (come on, we may not have done all the sins, but most of us have a favorite one like lying). The Golden Text of the Bible says it so simply, even a child can understand it:

> "For God so loved the world that He gave His only begotten Son that whoever believes in Him should not perish but have everlasting life. For God did not send His Son into the world to condemn the world, but that the world through Him might be saved. He who believes in Him is not condemned; but he who does not believe is condemned already, because he has not believed in the Name of the only begotten Son of God. And this is the condemnation, that the light has come into the world, and men loved darkness rather than light because their deeds were evil"
> John 3:16-19.

Get it? Love and life come from God. Hate and death come from Satan, as his followers proudly attest.

While God's free gift is eternal life, you earn death by your sins. You are not insane, are you? The choice is yours. His gracious love gifted you with the power to choose. I am holding my breath. I hope you choose life. It's a decision you make for your eternity.

Most people are born into a cultural religion so it's as innate to them as the color of their skin. However, religion is man trying to find God. That is why almost every tribe has its own god.

But God is not lost. God came from heaven through Jesus to look for lost man. While he lived on earth. Jesus demonstrated God's mercy, compassion, power and plan for us. He demonstrated how the humiliation and agony of dying was conquered by resurrection life. By this, He solved the mystery of death and removed its sting and fear.

Before He died on the cross, Jesus declared,

> "I am the way, the truth and the life. No man comes to the Father except through me."
>
> John 14:6

Every time you see a cross, let it remind you of the way to heaven.

A religious leader came to Jesus one night, and it is to him that Jesus said, "You must be born again." (John 3)

If your decision is to go to heaven, this simple prayer is the beginning of your born again life.

Dear Jesus,
Thank you for loving me just as I am.
I admit that I am a sinner and cannot save myself.
Thank you for dying on the Cross and taking

the punishment for me. Please forgive me of
all my sins and I invite you to be the Lord of my life.
Please guide me with your Holy Spirit, I pray,
in Jesus' name. Amen!

If you sincerely believed and said that prayer, you have been born into the kingdom of God. You are now part of the large family of God. You have relatives all over the world. Start your relationship by going to a church which believes in leading born again Christians into becoming disciples of Jesus Christ.

The accessibility of the Bible by most of the people of the world today, has proven that the power of its message is universally the same and true. Wherever you go in the world, Christians of all denominations have the same connection to the Creator, the same moral code, the same love for each other.

We have the same vision of sharing our wonderful faith and sharing life with the hurt and disenfranchised. We don't take advantage of them. We help them enjoy the privileges of their heavenly Father. We build hospitals, orphanages, safe homes for the abused. We help addicts recover. We help those in prison find new life. We feed the hungry. We build wells with clean water. We teach them how to pray and be dependent on Him for their need, developing a personal relationship with the Source of Life.

These and more may have been replicated by governments or rich humanitarians. But the idea of unselfish love is taught and sacrifices are made by simple individuals who want to be a part of God's plan for the entire world.

Jesus said that all the laws hang on two great ones.

"You shall love the Lord your God with all your
heart, with all your soul, and with all your mind.

This is the first and great commandment. And
the second is like it: You shall love your neighbor
as yourself."

Matthew 22:37-39.

Christian organizations go wrong and become like social
agencies when they get these commandments mixed up. We
make them happy here and fail to tell them how to get to heaven.

We must love God first and if we do, loving our neighbor as
ourselves will fall in place. God's plan is superior to socialism.
It is mandated by love and not forced by law.

All who are born again look forward to Jesus fulfilling His
promise to come again to take us to a place prepared for those
who believe in Him.

All believe that there are only two destinations after death...
heaven or hell. If the devil has made your short life on earth miserable, are you not insane to want to spend eternity with him?

All believe that each one chooses for himself the eternal destination of his afterlife. Choosing Jesus means choosing eternal
life. Refusing Jesus means choosing eternal death.

I recently heard a testimony that relates the wonderful
miraculous experience of the new birth. I heard Becket Cook
being interviewed and it is a perfect example of God's grace.

He came from a good family, nominally religious. When
he told his parents that he was gay, they were a bit taken aback,
but were loving and respected his decision. He thought he was
very happy living that lifestyle but as he got older and had experienced all the dreams, he had had for himself, he found himself very empty. One day as he was sitting with a friend, they
noticed that there was a group of people studying a Bible. He
was curious because he knew very little about the Bible. It made

him inquire about what they were doing. He didn't understand much but he was drawn to them.

They invited him to church the next Sunday. He heard the sermon and people prayed with him. It was not until later that he was thinking about what had been shared with him and he found himself wanting more. He was almost instantly changed from the inside when he asked Jesus to forgive him. As he stepped out of the church, he knew that he was no longer gay. Years of the homosexual lifestyle had left him with incredible emptiness. His story of the power of Jesus Christ changing him is told in his book: "A Change of Affection: A Gay Man's Incredible Story of Redemption." Look up Becket Cook's testimonies on YouTube and you will be amazed at the wonderful love and power of God.

We must love these who are hurting and want to come out of that lifestyle…and many are. Some have been "recruited", and our schools are teaching them lies that they have a choice. We were at a restaurant once when many started coming to have a "gay" nightclub after hours. One was a former student of mine. My friend and I started praying and the Lord told us to repent for not loving them as they are and labeling them. He gave them the gifts that they have and that they are very precious to Him. The Lord told us that many turned to gay friends because they were accepted there and felt rejection from us. I believe our repentance has allowed the Lord to trust us to minister to them. These are some websites that can help:

changemovement.com
www1.cbn.com
steam.org
www.christianpost.com

Jesus doesn't hate the sinner. He hates the sin that robs us of purpose and fulfillment. No matter what sin you have committed he can forgive all. Look over this list as found in Romans 1:29-31 and check your favorite:

___all unrighteousness
___sexual immorality
___wickedness
___covetousness
___maliciousness
___envy
___murder
___strife
___deceit
___evil mindedness
___whisperers
___backbiters
___haters of God
___violent
___proud
___boasters
___inventors of evil things
___disobedient to parents
___undiscerning
___untrustworthy
___unloving
___unforgiving
___unmerciful

The Good News (that's what gospel means) is that no matter how many you checked off, the Bible says that

> "If we confess our sins, He (Jesus) is faithful and
> just to forgive us our sins and to cleanse us from
> all unrighteousness."
>
> 1 John 1:9

And this is where we Pentecostals give a great big shout of hallelujah! We join the angels of heaven in rejoicing that your name is now written in God's Book of Life.

We have this powerful Gospel to declare to hurting people! God needs us!

This pandemic has revealed to us the need of God-fearing ones to stand united. We know Satan's tactic is to divide and conquer.

Satan's army has united against us. All those of us who believe in the Apostle's Creed should band together to defeat the enemy. Do you know that if all Americans who believe in the Bible's morality would register and vote, we could rule America? So, what's the problem?

I remember when I was a little girl and my mother and her two friends were new Christians, that whenever they met for coffee, each was subtly trying to get the other two to go to their church. Our church was called a Full Gospel Church. One lady was a Baptist and the other was a Seventh Day Adventist.

They admirably did not argue but I wondered if you became a Christian in a certain church, were you stuck forever? Of course, I silently sided with my mother since we were full gospel. I wondered why the others did not want to be full.

I know that Jesus said in Matthew 5:6,

> "Blessed are those who hunger and thirst for
> righteousness for they shall be filled."

I think I got my answer. He will fill us to our hunger and thirst level.

In my thirst to be full, I went to a Baptist seminary to get full. I got full of the word and the love they showed me.

I love going to Catholic or Episcopalian Christmas masses and appreciate so much the beauty of the liturgical celebration. I get full of the awe and wonder of the incarnation of God!

I take my leadership team every year to the statewide Hawaiian Islands Ministries Conference where the organized Presbyterians bring the best speakers and equippers to us to strengthen the whole body of Christ. We get really full.

In this urgent call to be united as the enemy against us is united, stop and embrace other Christian denominations that feel full where they are and appreciate their fulness. We don't need to argue our differences but celebrate each others' strengths.

I love Pastor Che Ahn for his leadership in the important prayer Movement for our country.

I love the strong contemporary preaching of Pastor Jack Hibbs. He is relevant and yet so Biblically focused on the message of the Cross.

I love the teaching of Dr. David Jeremiah, especially his teachings on the End Times.

I love J.D. Farag's "prophecy updates" program which simply and profoundly explain how today's news stories are fulfilling Biblical prophecy.

I love the preaching of Dr. John Hagee who keeps us tied to the nation of Israel and the blessing of Abraham! I love to see generations building the kingdom of God as his family has.

I love all the Messianic Rabbis. They help me understand the whole Bible better. They connect us to the Jewish traditions and help us to relate to the characters of the Bible.

I love the teachings of Pastor Robert Morris. His humor and practical illustrations are realistic and helpful.

I love the multi-faceted ministry of Pat Robertson: his daily inspirational program, The 700 Club, his university which trains graduates for positions of leadership for our country, his outreach through Operation Blessing to help needy people worldwide. His impeccable character and steady leadership are a great example to all Christian leaders.

I totally love Joyce Meyers. Her practical teachings have inspired millions. Being a woman in this mixed up world, she has shown how a godly woman can stay under the covering of a Christian husband who has a bad case of masculinity and both build up the Kingdom of God....no competition but cooperating with the Holy Spirit to bring glory to God.

I love my Catholic friends (I think they are still hoping that I will become a nun). I watch their pro-life programs. Their teachings on family, pro-creation and the sanctity of sex and your body is what Protestants need to hear.

I have heard someone in the Protestant circle say that Protestants are against abortion until their daughter gets pregnant out of wedlock. I know mothers who unashamedly give their teenage daughters birth control pills instead of teaching them abstinence until marriage. When Christians join the ungodly to view sex as recreational rather than procreational, we spawn problems like abortion and birth control mechanisms. The trend of Protestants has been to limit the number of children and most of the time it is because they feel that they cannot afford more than two. That is so unbiblical because God said to multiply, and He promises over and over to supply our needs. We have fallen into the trap of most godless Americans that providing material things are more important than being in the will of God and trusting Him to keep His promises.

One of my crazy courageous team members is Dr. Andrew Kayes. He ran for office when he heard that Hawaii was about to pass the physician assisted end-of-life bill. His Catholic parents had three children and then adopted 16 physically challenged children from Europe and Asia. I told him that they must be very wealthy. He said, "No, but they always had faith that God would allow them to do what was needed and would supply their needs. These parents inspire me and are heroes to me.

Let's repent and be humble and learn from the Catholics and truly be pro-life.

I love Steve Furtick. I pray for his wife. With all that energy on stage, I wonder if he helps with chores. I wish I could keep my congregation awake as he does.

I love Joni's talk show because she lets the guest talk more and her subjects are tough and relevant. I love their beautiful family.

I love Sid Roth because he challenges me to continue to hunger and thirst after God. I have a couple in my church who are amputees. I told them to ask God to help them believe that their limbs would grow again. I hear these amazing stories on his programs and stay hungry for more....and I am experiencing some wonderful miracles myself.

I know you have your favorite preachers, too. They're more whom I love and respect but I like to recommend these as starters.

Let's give everyone the freedom to be full of God, wherever their hunger level is.

We need everyone with whatever faith we have to stand against our common enemy, the devil.

In trying to promote unity, I have planted seeds for each island to have an "I Love America" (John Peterson) choir where all Christians can stand together for our country. The local

Catholic priest and I meet some of the choir members every Tuesday for lunch to fellowship and pray. I think I can hear the angels singing, "Behold, how good and how pleasant it is for brethren to dwell together in unity." (Psalm 133:1).

In this urgent time when our country is about to implode, I believe pastors and other spiritual leaders must lead the charge.

God is on our side. He has given us His promises. We always use 2 Chronicles 7:14 as a call to prayer for our nation.

> "If my people who are called by My name will humble themselves, and pray and seek My face, and turn from their wicked ways, then I will hear from heaven, and will forgive their sin and heal their land."

Are we waiting for Him to answer our prayers? I think He is waiting for us to humble ourselves and turn from our wicked ways.

If we believe that only the Spirit of God can save our nation, then we must begin with repentance. I think we have failed to preach it enough. But, more than that, we have failed to practice it ourselves for parishioners to see.

Could we humble ourselves and ask Him to forgive us for breaking The Ten Commandments?

1. You shall have no other gods before me. Have you made the reputation of your church or ministry more important than doing His will?
2. You shall not make for yourself a carved image…you shall not bow to them or serve them. Are you bowing to your Board or your financial supporters or to God alone?

3. You shall not take the name of the Lord your God in vain. Have you ever said, "God told me", when He didn't?
4. Remember the Sabbath Day, to keep it holy? Do you try to redefine this or are you able to rest as He did and realize that you are not indispensable?
5. Honor your father and your mother. Do you? Are you thankful and do you honor anyone who helped you become who you are?
6. You shall not murder. Do you hate your critics, or do you learn from them?
7. You shall not commit adultery. What about pornography or infidelity in your heart?
8. You shall not steal. Did you steal some sheep from another pastor?
9. You shall not bear false witness against your neighbor. Have you defamed or unfairly criticized another pastor?
10. You shall not covet your neighbor's house or church; you shall not covet your neighbor's wife, nor his male staff nor his female staff, nor his car or anything that is your neighbor's. Plead guilty?

I don't want to expose all that I have seen and heard but the American church is rife with competing, compromising and comparing. Unless we spiritual leaders lead in repentance and humility, it is futile for us to call people to pray and expect the promise of 2 Chronicles 7 to be fulfilled.

We are called ministers and we must serve. We are called leaders and we must lead. We are called Christians and we must be Christlike.

When we humble ourselves before God, He will use us to lead our country back to Him.

"The eyes of the Lord are on the righteous, and His ears are open to their cry. The face of the Lord is against those who do evil, to cut off the remembrance of them from the earth. The righteous cry out, and the Lord hears, and delivers them out of all their troubles. The Lord is near to those who have a broken heart, and saves such as have a contrite spirit.

Psalm 34: 15-18

This election is pivotal to our future. In light of Biblical prophecy, I believe God set this country up to spread the gospel around the world. He allowed our Nation to be birthed and kept us alive for nearly 300 years. Up to this generation, we have sent out more missionaries than any other country. But now missionaries are coming from other countries to evangelize us. Is our time over?

Many believe that there will be one last harvest before Jesus comes again. I believe that it can happen if we unite and work hard to defeat the enemy who has shown his ugly head.

Because this election in Hawaii will be by mail-in votes (I don't know whose crazy idea that was), I am urging pastors to have a registration Sunday and then election Sunday when everybody brings his ballot and vote together. Pastors need to inform their congregants of the Godly candidates...and there are some in both parties.

Although Hawaii's political past is dismal, with God, I am hopeful He is a God of miracles. Just before last year's state Republican convention on Maui, I had the craziest miracle.

I have a house dress that is about 10 years old. I wear it when I am piddling around the kitchen. I throw it in the wash with my dish towels and aprons. One day when I pulled the load out of the dryer and began to fold them, I had 2 of the same dress. I stared at them and wondered what was going on. I told the Lord, "Of all the miracles I have experienced, this is the craziest. What is the meaning of this?"

For three days He didn't answer. On the third day as I was praying and still wondering, He said, "You have always quoted Ephesians 3:20,21....

> 'Now to Him who is able to do exceedingly abun-
> dantly above all that we ask or think, according
> to the power that works in us...to Him be glory
> in the church by Christ Jesus to all generations,
> forever and ever. Amen.'

I have given you this to show those who need a miracle or who don't believe in miracles."

Be careful when you stay hungry for more of God. It will make you look like you are crazy. But we are not going to get things done in our nation if we are not willing be to crazier than the white-clad angry insane ladies and their ferocious leader.

The Lord told me to wear that old dress and carry the miracle one in a bag when I was asked to give the invocation at the state Republican Convention being held on Maui. I thought it was a crazy idea but I obeyed. They also wanted me to pray for one of our former U.S. Representatives who was very ill.

I did and told them that if they would believe what I shared, God can give us victory. (the person we prayed for called me to thank me and said that she felt something happened even though she was not present and that she had a very good report from the doctor.)

So, I want all who need a miracle and who would like to join me for a miracle for this country to become great again, join the crazy courageous like me, and let us see God do it!!!

Like the two old sisters in the islands of the Hebrides, there are two old sisters on this Pacific island of Maui (my sister June, the prayer warrior and me, the writer) who are praying for God to save our nation!

I have two goals. The first is to get all Christians to display their moral conscience and help Godly people get elected. There are Godly people in both parties because some want to make changes from within their party. One thing I would not compromise on is the right for the unborn baby to have the right to life, liberty and the pursuit of happiness. They have no voice so I feel we have to speak for them and that would be the test a candidate would have to pass. It will reveal his moral character.

I want each to register to vote, learn about the candidates and go out and vote…..and influence five friends to go with you.

The other one is to inspire choirs and choral groups everywhere to take John Peterson's timeless musical "I love America" to every mall and political event. We need to stir up the airwaves countering the hateful chants of the godless. There are three sections which should speak for itself:

1. Patriotism for America
2. Praise for America
3. Prayer for America

If twelve, yes, twelve crazy courageous could do it on the stage of the biggest mall on Maui, you can do it in your town or city. I believe music carries the anointing of the Holy Spirit. It can change the atmosphere of your city and can change the atmosphere of our nation. Try it! You'll love it!! I like making God laugh His holy laughter!!

I think if we can get churches to organize like the trade unions do, it will be a start. They recruit volunteers, have fundraisers, go door-to-door, be sure everyone is registered and then take them to the polling place. That's how their candidates win.

The Catholic channel EWTN has an excellent pro-life program and you can go to their website: prolifeweekly.com

The Family Research Council may be able to educate you about candidates.

Look, nowadays it seems everybody is crazy. I know there are other crazy (about our country) courageous like me who will join our crazy courageous leader and win!!! Let's flutter our butterfly wings together and cause a hurricane victory for our nation.

If you are not ashamed to be affiliated with us and are tough enough to withstand the intimidating name calling, you qualify to join us.

ORDER YOUR UNIFORM FROM

MAUICUSTOMT-SHIRTS.COM
$16 per shirt
God bless you and God bless America!

CPSIA information can be obtained
at www.ICGtesting.com
Printed in the USA
LVHW071758120521
687225LV00017B/605